DIVERSITY FOR FUN AND PROFIT

DIVERSITY FOR FUN AND PROFIT

ETHAN S. SHAPIRO

© 2017 Ethan S. Shapiro
All rights reserved.

ISBN-13: 9781540397652
ISBN-10: 1540397653
Library of Congress Control Number: 2016919066
CreateSpace Independent Publishing Platform
North Charleston, South Carolina

DEDICATION

* For Jane, who has always been there in so many ways
* Jonas and Lulu who teach me every day about the joy in life
* Mom and Dad who taught me to be principled and moral
* Mark, Marla & the UBI associates who educated me about the communities

TABLE OF CONTENTS

Why Diversity ····································ix

Chapter 1 In the Beginning; Me, Me, Me················ 1
Chapter 2 Kumbaya ································· 8
Chapter 3 Times Are Changing····················· 30
Chapter 4 We Can't Find Any of Those ················ 41
Chapter 5 Why Create a Diverse Workplace ············ 49
Chapter 6 The Benefits of Diverse Ages and
           Genders in the Workplace················· 65
Chapter 7 The ABCs of LGBTQ ···················· 73
Chapter 8 Understanding the Diverse Customer—
           Inclusion as a Driver of Business ············ 89
Chapter 9 The American Way, the Corporate Way,
           the Political Way······················· 100
Chapter 10 Aye-Aye, Sir…Er, Ma'am The Elements for
           Building a Diverse Workforce and Culture···· 127
Chapter 11 On Immigrants—Welcome, Now Please Go ····142
Chapter 12 Why the Word "Minority" Lowers
           Expectations ························ 152

Inspiration ·161
Addendum ·163
Songs ·175
Endnotes ·177

WHY DIVERSITY

In understanding and recruiting people from diverse environments and experiences, businesses can be more effective in marketing to potential customers that come from various racial and cultural backgrounds, including women and members of the LBGTQ community. By recruiting from a larger and diverse pool of candidates, businesses increase the odds of attracting the best and the brightest. Talent acquisition has become crucial in positively affecting the bottom line and understanding how to appeal to the most diverse group of applicants has become vital for success in the marketplace. Bringing together workers with distinctive qualifications, backgrounds, and experiences enhance effective problem-solving on the job.

Diversity in the workplace and communities has become a hot topic in the American media, offices and factories. It is the subject of dozens of workshops and training sessions being run every day at seminars and companies across the country. The topic is covered on social media sites, magazines, blogs, and in newspapers every week. Even so, trying to force diversity in American companies can cause consternation and frustration in human resources offices as well as at the desks of those creating résumés for job searches. While companies attempt to state their diverse makeup in public relations (PR) materials many feature organizational photos depicting primarily white males blurring the value to the company and prospective hires. So, while companies claim they are seeking a more diverse workforce, they should understand diversity or lack of it may be most apparent and out front for all to see. The diversity of a company must be marketed, initially within the organization so the word gets out that company is a good place for everyone to work. Then, to effectively market to a diverse customer base, a business must understand how to build a company that represents the customers. Leadership is often unsure of how to go about creating and managing workforces that reflect the populations they serve while not becoming too insular or out of touch. It is easy to recruit surface diversity based on sex, age and race but developing productive teams committed to working together requires skills and a commitment from leadership and the workforce. I do not believe conventional diversity programs and training are effective although many companies have them in place to protect themselves from litigation and to satisfy a company requirement to have a program. Why these programs don't work are varied and complex, most are designed to police people's thoughts and force feed the "right" thoughts and actions. This does not work as we are all biased in certain ways and shamming and disapproval can cause a backlash and have a negative effect on the individuals and the group. For many companies, efforts to create a workforce that looks like the target audience backfires, failing and costing a great deal of money, time, and often the retention of valued workers. For many corporate diversity managers, designing hiring practices to attract and retain minorities and implementing programs to create more sensitive and tolerant workplaces are just public relations maneuvers. *Look how diverse we are! Buy our products and use our services because we employ people who look like you!* After companies, have spent a great deal of energy researching and implementing programs designed on often confusing objectives to determine what a diverse workplace should look like, they fall short in having the employees understand that diverse associates are not hired simply for diversity purposes but for specific skills. The entire group must be cohesive and must feel a part of the process and realize they all benefit from the collaborative effort.

Americans are generally not comfortable with the unfamiliar, and for many, minorities and others who don't look or act as they do are mysterious and even a little scary. Many believe racial attitudes have regressed, and our leaders in society and government don't seem to have the capability or determination to address these problems socially or by legislation. This makes it even more difficult for management at companies where in some cases, employees have expressed outright fear of working with someone who looks and sounds different from them.

It is commonly accepted that prejudice has different points of origin; chief among them is fear. How to overcome these fears and make associates dependent on diversity for their success is the focal point of the book. I believe there is a practical way to approach diversity training and depending on the average programs and manuals isn't the way and doesn't work because there is no average workplace. Your program must be designed to fulfill the needs of your business and your customers. *Diversity for Fun and Profit* seeks to educate those who want to create an environment that reflects that population but doesn't force the issue for PR brownie points.

Chapter 1

IN THE BEGINNING; ME, ME, ME

"Ah, Sweet Mystery of Life"
Jeanette MacDonald, Nelson Eddy

> Ah! Sweet mystery of life
> At last I've found thee
> Ah! I know at last the secret of it all;
> All the longing, seeking, striving, waiting, yearning
> The burning hopes, the joy and idle tears that fall!
> For 'tis love, and love alone, the world is seeking,
> And 'tis love, and love alone, that can repay!
> 'Tis the answer, 'tis the end and all of living

When I was growing up, I lived in a neighborhood, a real neighborhood, in a small town in rural Pennsylvania. I am Jewish and was a minority, but even so, my family and I were always part of the community. My dad was one of a few doctors in town and was not only essential to the populace but beloved for his kindness and generosity. There was certainly anti-Semitism, but folks relied on my father and realized he made their lives better so he was "forgiven" for being a Jew. Most people who knew us accepted us and our religion—what little they understood. As time, progressed, more doctors came to town, and my father, along with his peers, was instrumental in enlarging the hospital and providing local care equal to that of the nearby cities. Although they had different backgrounds, both ethnic and religious, and were different genders, the physicians all had medicine in common and needed one another to be successful and to provide the best care to the town.

In my neighborhood and at my school—unlike in cities, where ethnic groups usually lived together in somewhat self-imposed ghettos of Irish, Italian, German, and so on—we lived, studied, and played together or at least nearby. The friends I made in kindergarten are, all these years later, still some of my closest friends. What bound us together was age and community, although so much else about us was different. I remember an assignment we were given in elementary school to prepare a report about our heritage and the countries from which our families immigrated. I believe I was the only one with Russia in my background, and I took a lot of good-natured ribbing, as it was the late-Stalin / early-Khrushchev years and we were all united against our Cold War enemy. My young fifth-grade classmates were fascinated by the fact that my grandparents had to flee the country under assumed identities to safely come to America, although there seemed to be a lot of confusion about the czars and the Russian Communists. The point is that as children, we were all united against our common enemy, Communism, and regardless of our backgrounds, which were very diverse, we behaved as one. Economically and ethnically, the neighborhood families were distinct in religion, education, vocation, and origin. Our black classmates rarely discussed their experiences and our teachers seldom taught us about slavery.

Segregation in all its various shapes was institutionalized in the 1950s, though we were blindly unaware. Yet we as children, though not most parents, socialized and played together, for if we hadn't, there would have been no games or social life. We never thought about needing one another, but that is what it was. Certainly, some were better athletes, students, speakers, musicians, and so on, but being part of a group, a neighborhood team, made us stronger, better balanced and more competitive allowing us to win more games and do well as individuals. Diversity comes down to one question: Are groups or individuals with varied levels of skill better at optimally performing? Are forming teams of diverse groups of people with a blend of backgrounds, ideas, and personalities better suited to performing better than individuals.

In terms of their characteristics, lifestyles, and attitudes, boomers like me have defined themselves by their careers, and many are workaholics,[1] but many of us were also the generation that fought for civil rights in the 1960s. As for generation X, generation Y (the millennials), and generation Z, although these younger generations profess a lack of prejudice, they have not spent time living with people unlike themselves. If you investigate cultures where group efforts are highly valued, you might find that in many of them, that is the case only when the groups comprise those with similar physical and social status. Otherwise, prejudice would restrict and restrain diversity.[2] "In healthy societies, people live their lives within a galaxy of warm places. They are members of a family, neighborhood, school, civic organization, hobby group, company, faith, regional culture, nation, continent and world. Each layer of life is nestled in the others to form a varied but coherent whole."[3]

When I was growing up in the 1950s and 1960s, we didn't realize we had prejudices, at least not in my house. We were taught by our parents to respect our elders, and never was that respect tinged by color or religion. What I now realize, although I believed I was raised in what I consider a prejudice-free house, is that it was prejudice-free for the times. I was a second-generation American, and we lived in a multigenerational home: grandparents escaping from the shtetls of Europe, parents facing anti-Semitism and quotas to gain admission to college[4] and, in my father's case, medical school, although he was a straight A student with two PhDs. I still have the letters he received stating that his application was too late and the two spots for Jews had been filled.

As a youth and visiting nearby Baltimore, I saw the signs at the public pools: "No Jews, no Negroes, and no dogs.On a family vacation to Williamsburg, Virginia, to learn about colonial America, I observed the "colored" water fountains and bathrooms and found this all very confusing, as I had "Negroes" as school friends, and we all shared bathrooms. After the trip, I did begin to question whether the "colored" sat in the balcony at our town movie theater just because it was more fun. And then, I couldn't remember any black kids going to the pool, except the YMCA. How often did we go to each other's homes? Sometimes, but not often, and rarely for a sleepover. It was the beginning of my awareness of civil rights.

Being Jewish and growing up less than twenty years after the Holocaust, my sister and I acquired, from our grandparents, a distrust and apprehension of anyone who wasn't Jewish and a kinship to anyone who was. My best friend from my youth was Jewish, and when we were together I felt more comfortable and emotionally safe, free from jokes and putdowns. Our grandparents and parents slipped into Yiddish anytime they wanted to speak disparagingly of others and didn't think my sister or I would understand. It didn't take us long to define schwartze, shiksa, shegetz, goy, yutz, and mensch.[5] We were always aware of being Jewish and being different;

my grandmother called anyone not Jewish a stranger, meaning "not to be trusted." Although my grandparents were Orthodox, our one and only synagogue joined the Conservative movement to accommodate Jewish families moving into the community. The synagogue, Congregation Sons of Israel, founded in 1919 by my grandfather and others of his generation, is still in existence. It was difficult living a double life—one that most people I knew had no idea existed. Our town was in the Pennsylvania Dutch country and quite insular. But for the most part, the people were good people, especially after my father became accepted and came to be a much-admired town doctor.

Growing up in the 1950s and 1960s was much less complex and seemingly less problematic than today's world, so I never really thought there was overt racism or prejudice in my town. Like my fellow Jews, we congregants knew we were different, accepted what went along with that difference, and believed, only among ourselves of course, in our superiority to the goyim or non-Jews. What we didn't understand was that this was a device used to protect ourselves from the anti-Semitism we experienced although it was less explicit than previous generations suffered. Just as we Jews hid behind our shields of concealed condescension, the Negroes knew they had no choice but to be second-class citizens, as institutionalized racism was a way of life and, depending on where one lived, could be more punitive or more accommodating.

We must recognize that "racism was originally built into the US legal system as white supremacy was among the values the 'founding fathers' were trying to preserve. As institutions were built alongside the building of the US legal system, racism and its underlying racial ideologies were built into the laws and built into the institutions."[6] Is it any wonder that, although markedly improved, racism continues to be a way of life in the United States? Perhaps this assessment is a bit unfair, but the dialog by many on the "alt-right" or "alternative right" seems to be exemplifying the "me first" attitude, which is disturbing in that perhaps up to half the population of the United States shares this view. Some of the biggest proponents of "Me, Me, and Me" are Rush Limbaugh, who refers to himself as America's anchorman, President Donald Trump, who says, "I feel a lot of people listen to what I have to say," Laura Ingraham, who said, "The viler the things that're said about me, the less it affects me. It doesn't bother me at all," and Ann Coulter, who is quoted as saying, "I love to engage in repartee with people who are stupider than I am." With so many more politicians of both parties, celebrities, and sports figures whose most inane comments are broadcast on social media, is it any wonder that this attitude of entitlement slips into the workplace, causing divisiveness and discord?

In any typical diversity training program, this subject is never brought up, but managers must be aware and aggressive in an ever more polarizing society. In the workplace, diverse ideas lead to creative solutions, but opposing factions can lead to a war inside a company and are a main cause of an unproductive environment. Owing to the ease of social media, people with no real "expertise now pass as legitimate spokespeople or learned analysts. They write about their theories and assumptions as if they were facts. These then are recirculated, as legitimate news and people recount these theories and demand answers without pausing to consider if there's a basis for the question."[7] These observations and fake news stories reinforce stereotypes, and managers must be trained to act as mediators and sit people down and have them listen to one another.

"Conflicts in the workplace resulting from people locking horns with each other due to their divergent perspectives can be resolved if the parties are willing to join in a search for greater mutual understanding of each other's viewpoints. The more willing they are to examine and test their assumptions against more objectively based evidence, the greater the hope that they can use the mediation process to resolve their conflicts peacefully and to work together effectively."[8] It is exciting when one is enthusiastic and passionate about an idea or a position, but if it slips into extremism, the viewpoint can become more entrenched and extreme. Conflict has the potential to promote creativity and innovation, but it is also a significant contributing factor to low workplace morale, employee disengagement, stress, and physical illness. Left unaddressed, conflict can have a devastating effect on the work environment.

Chapter 2

● ● ●

KUMBAYA

Kumbaya[9] means "come by here" in Gullah, an African American dialect that originated in the coastal regions of South Carolina and Georgia. This song is believed to have been written in the 1930s, but it enjoyed a resurgence during the 1960s and remains a classic campfire song. It was originally associated with human and spiritual unity, closeness, and compassion for one another.

> *Kum bay ya, my Lord, kum bay ya;*
> *Kum bay ya, the Lord, kum bay ya;*
> *Kum bay ya, my Lord, kum bay ya,*
> *O Lord, kum bay ya.*

Let's all hold hands and sing "Kumbaya" together! OK, well, maybe around the campfire with the Boy Scout troop, but please not in the conference room at work! Though the song is meaningful and bears an important message for all citizens of the world, it does not and cannot apply to diversity in the workplace.

Diversity is not a song or about holding hands or group hugs. It is not warm and fuzzy feelings generated by forced diversity-orientation programs, motivational meetings, or corporate hiring directives. Most corporate training programs and seminars delivered by self-proclaimed diversity experts are a waste of time and money and, frankly, are painful to participate in. Billions of hours and dollars are spent to diversify America's companies, but the programs rarely work, and no one can explain why. Government programs, like the Equal Employment Opportunity Commission (EEOC), exist to prevent discrimination in the workplace but not to encourage diversity.

The EEOC came into being through Title VII of the Civil Rights Act of 1964. This included the provisions that a person cannot be discriminated against for employment based on race, sex, religion, color, national origin, and/or disability. Recent amendments to the original law include the Americans with Disabilities Act Amendments of 2008 and the Genetic Information Nondiscrimination Act of 2008. Some states and local governments extend protections to other categories, such as marital status, sexual preference, genetics, and other classifications. Title VII and its amendments, additional regulations, and add-ons over forty-five years have allowed for the creation of one of the largest growth industries in corporate history, and yet most studies reveal that years of work are needed to create workplaces that are truly conscious of the law's requirements.[10]

Someone's laughing, Lord, kum bay ya;
Someone's laughing, Lord, kum bay ya;
Someone's laughing, Lord, kum bay ya,
O Lord, kum bay ya.

To understand what diversity looks like, we need to understand what is a minority and what is discrimination based on minority status per the EEOC:[11]

* The law forbids discrimination when it comes to any aspect of employment, including hiring, firing, pay, job assignment, promotion, layoff, training, fringe benefits, and any other term or condition of employment
* The law forbids treating someone unfavorably because that person is of a certain race or because of personal characteristics associated with race (such as hair texture, skin color, or certain facial features). Color discrimination involves treating someone unfavorably because of skin color.)
* Race/color discrimination also can involve treating someone unfavorably because the person is married to (or associated with) a person of a certain race or color or because of a person's connection with a race-based organization or group, or an organization or group that is generally associated with people of a certain color.
* Discrimination can occur when the victim and the person who inflicted the discrimination are the same race or color

SOME COMMON DEFINITIONS OF MINORITIES AND DISCRIMINATION

* Racial or ethnic minority: A racial or ethnic minority is a human group having racial, religious, linguistic, and certain other traits in common. A group of people of common ancestry, distinguished from others by physical characteristics such as hair type, color of eyes and skin, stature, and so on.
* Gender and sexual discrimination: Sexual discrimination involves treating someone (an applicant or employee) unfavorably because of that person's gender. Sexual discrimination also can involve treating someone less favorably because

of his or her connection with an organization or group that is generally associated with people of a certain gender.
* Religious discrimination: Religious discrimination involves treating a person (an applicant or employee) unfavorably because of his or her religious beliefs. The law protects people who belong to traditional, organized religions, such as Buddhism, Christianity, Hinduism, Islam, and Judaism, and others who have sincerely held religious, ethical, or moral beliefs.
* Age discrimination: The Age Discrimination in Employment Act (ADEA) forbids only age discrimination against people who are age forty or older. It does not protect workers under the age of forty, although some states do have laws that protect younger workers from age discrimination.

Disability discrimination: disability discrimination occurs when an employer or other entity covered by the American with Disabilities Act, as amended, or the Rehabilitation Act, as amended, treats a qualified individual with a disability who is an employee or applicant unfavorably because he or she has a disability. Disability discrimination also occurs when an employee treats an applicant or employee less favorably because he or she has a history of a disability (such as cancer that is controlled or in remission) or because he or she is believed to have a physical or mental impairment that is not transitory (lasting or expected to last six months or less) and minor (even if he or she does not have such an impairment). The law requires an employer to provide reasonable accommodation to an employee or job applicant with a disability, unless doing so would cause significant difficulty or expense for the employer ("undue hardship"). The law also protects people from discrimination based on their relationship with a person with a disability (even if they do not themselves have a disability). For example, per the US Equal Employment Opportunity Commission and the Americans with Disabilities Act, it is illegal to discriminate against an employee because his or her spouse has a disability.

A FEW DETAILS ABOUT DIVERSITY AND THE DIVERSITY INDUSTRY[12]

* If you Google "diversity" you will get about 385,000 thousand hits in the first second.
* There are over one million diversity consultants and firms in the United States, as evidenced by the professional organizations to which many of them belong. These include the Association of Law Firm Diversity Professionals, Alliance of Supplier Diversity Professionals, the Professional and Technical Diversity Network, and the Alliance for Board Diversity, to name just a few.
* There is a magazine titled *Diversity Officer Magazine* and an academic institution called Diversity Training University International.
* The average salary of a diversity officer at a Fortune 500 company is $225,000, not including annual bonuses.
* The average budget for a diversity office at a Fortune 500 company is almost $3 million.
* There are thousands of diversity conferences per year across the country.
* The EEOC presented an operating budget of more than $373 million for 2016.[13] There are thousands of firms nationwide charging millions of dollars just to interpret the laws and directives of the EEOC. There are countless lobbyists in Washington and every state capital

representing the interests of those who seek diversity in companies large and small. The concept they promote is designed to make those who are implementing diversity practices feel good about throwing their dollars at the idea, as well as to make those who don't devote human resources and budget dollars feel guilty, as if they were somehow not perpetuating the Great American Dream. Diversity is a growth industry and is constantly changing, requiring even more manpower and dollars to stay abreast of changes and innovations. But it just doesn't seem to work. We know now that the private sector is obsessed with making the "Most Hospitable to Minorities and Women" lists published by various media during any given year.

It is possible that there isn't much difference between the money budgeted to marketing to a diverse customer base and the money budgeted to creating a workforce that looks like the customers. But what we don't know is how and why the US federal government spends so much to promote and enforce diversity. Typical or traditional diversity programs hurt the bottom line in the private sector as well as in the federal government.

Someone's crying, Lord, kum bay ya;
Someone's crying, Lord, kum bay ya;
Someone's crying, Lord, kum bay ya,
O Lord, kum bay ya.

Businesses are focused on training diversity professionals: You can now earn a degree in diversity, leading to a career in…

diversity! Here are a few of the degrees that can be earned with coursework and a concentration in diversity:

* AS, ethnic and diversity studies
* BA, gender and diversity studies
* MA, intercultural studies
* MA, bicultural-bilingual studies
* Bilingual Education and Diversity Studies Certification Program
* MA, bilingual education and diversity studies
* Even the US Military Academy at West Point offers degree programs in intercultural-multicultural and diversity studies, as do MIT, Columbia, Northwestern, UC Berkeley, Cornell, and many other top schools in the country.

In total, there are over four thousand institutions offering program to train students in the ambiguous topic of diversity. What are these students learning so that they can bring diversity to an American company or the American government? Many members of the faculty who teach these classes are called experts in multiculturalism, interculturalist, and diversity. How does one go about achieving that status? Many have no real business experience in a corporate setting and little firsthand understanding of how a corporation works in terms of operations or human resources. They may have backgrounds in government, academia, social work, psychology, or religion but have never had to make a payroll, generate revenue, or make a profit. I have great respect for academia and use research generated by university experts, but research is not business, and the qualifications for each differ greatly. In academia, you work within your field and with people who are like minded. In business, assumptions differ, as do backgrounds, causing the need for compromise when people may disagree. There are complications to deal with and basics and procedures that cannot be overlooked. In business speed is often of the essence.

Here are some titles now used in the corporate and academic world that didn't exist twenty years ago:

* Manager of diversity
* Director of diversity
* Diversity specialist
* Diversity educator
* Senior director, diversity and talent management
* Vice president of diversity
* Chief diversity officer (CDO)
* Diversity source and program manager
* Dean, associate and assistant dean for diversity and inclusion
* Assistant/associate director, Office of Institutional Equity and Diversity
* Diversity program coordinator and assistant coordinator for program project support
* Diversity manager/executive staffing
* Global diversity manager
* Special counsel diversity
* Diversity training and development manager
* Manager inclusive programming

And these are just a few of the titles and jobs! The diversity business is big business. I have no hard statistics to back up this theory, but I have attended dozens of diversity meetings and conventions, and ironically, it seems to me that many of these managers are minorities; African American, Hispanic and Asian. One might say the diversity field lacks diversity. Diversity experts often express frustration and aggravation in papers delivered at conferences and in books on the topic. They are mystified by the slow pace of change in corporate America and wonder why, with the significant resources, both human and financial, designated for diversity programs, there is so little progress.

Someone's praying, Lord, kum bay ya;
Someone's praying, Lord, kum bay ya;
Someone's praying, Lord, kum bay ya,
O Lord, kum bay ya.

One of the most interesting aspects of diversity is that almost every American is a member of some group that is recognized as part of a diverse group. If "minority" is defined as "a group of people who differ racially or politically from a larger group of which it is a part" or "being or relating to the smaller in number of two parts," then we all qualify in some way.[14] The EEOC classifies minorities in this way: [15]

* An American Indian or Alaskan Native is a person having origins in any of the original peoples of North America and who maintains his or her culture through a tribe or community.
* An Asian or Pacific Islander is a person having origins in any of the original people of the Far East, Southeast Asia, India, or the Pacific Islands. These areas include, for example, China, India, Korea, the Philippine Islands, and Samoa.
* A black (except Hispanic) person is a person having origins in any of the black racial groups of Africa.

* A Hispanic person is a person of Mexican, Puerto Rican, Cuban, Central or South American, or other Spanish culture or origin, regardless of race[15]

The population with origins in Europe, North Africa, or the Middle East makes up the dominant white population of the United States. Of course, many more minority groups can be identified in the American population. However, they are not classified separately as minorities under EEOC law. It should be noted that women are not classified as a minority. However, they have experienced the same kind of systematic exclusion from the economy as classified minorities have. Thus, they are considered as having minority status as far as the law is concerned.

I could go on indefinitely, defining who is protected under law, who is protected in certain businesses, universities, municipalities, and other entities. It seems that most of us are minorities in some way, therefore, what is a non-minority? The EEOC defines a non-minority as someone who is not an ethnic minority, has the same rights as "minorities" and are equally protected against discrimination. I assume that would make a white male a non-minority, but am I right or wrong? I have done hours of research trying to define a non-minority and cannot come up with a clear definition exclusive of countless exceptions. If a person is of European ancestry but is shorter than average or gay or physically disabled or intellectually disabled or obese, or he or she wears a headscarf, a skull cap or other accoutrement in consideration of his or her religion, aren't they still a potential target of discrimination? Is the person protected in the workplace from being overlooked for promotion or subject to ridicule or abuse? Not really. There are dozens of publications that annually list the best companies for minorities to work for. But these lists don't tell us what kinds of jobs these individuals hold and what the salaries are. So, the term "minority" might be accurate regarding an individual in a member of a group with a smaller number of people in it than the balance of that group. But it does not accurately reflect income level, level of authority and responsibility in a company, or potential opportunities for people to move into more senior positions.

There is so much confusing, hard-to-interpret data that it is no surprise many companies would rather just give up. They would rather not spend the money designing programs that, in my opinion, most of the time will not be effective or add to the company's bottom line but will instead cause confusion. If they choose to leave a "diversity position" in place—and most companies do for fear of appearing insensitive to diversity if they don't have one—it is often left only to placate HR people and make the company look as if it were doing something to create a more varied workplace.

Even the word "minority" has come to mean something almost negative—less powerful, less well represented, and without the same authority as the majority, per Melba Vasquez *The Ethnic and Racial Disparities in Education*, a report for the American Psychological Association. [16] The United States has always had a White majority but the Census Bureau projects that by 2040 White people will make up less than 50% of the population with the remainder comprised of multiple minorities. White people have historically held the power but that is about to change.

Barack Obama's 2008 election was thought to have heralded that change but with the election of Donald Trump it appears those factors are not as clear as we thought as he was elected by a white majority. Per the website, Fusion the most diverse counties in the US went for Hilary Clinton while the least diverse counties for Donald Trump. I believe Donald Trump was elected by the portion of the population that is uncomfortable living among a more diverse population. This may change as the minority population expands and may just be a glitch as we reach 2040 and a majority minority population. Still understanding diversity remains a key to understanding the future and how diversity will be accepted and accomplished as we are a nation of the self-interested and are subconsciously focused on self-preservation. We tend to draw those close to us and even closer in good times and bad; we reach out to family, neighbors, communities and houses of worship. We are not programmed to be a diverse society. We were not designed to seek diversity; rather, we were designed for survival and to seek the power of the pack.

Someone's singing, Lord, kum bay ya;
Someone's singing, Lord, kum bay ya;
Someone's singing, Lord, kum bay ya,
O Lord, kum bay ya.

Man, has been a tribal animal since he first walked erect, more than four million years ago and for two million years, the early hominid was a herd/tribal animal, primarily a herd herbivore. During the next two million years, man was a tribal hunter/warrior and still is. Human social drivers developed long before we developed intellectually. They are, therefore, instinctive. Such instincts as mother love, compassion, cooperation, curiosity, inventiveness, and competitiveness are ancient and embedded in the human psyche. They were all necessary for the survival of the human and pre-human. Since human social drives are instinctive (not intellectual), they cannot be modified through education (presentation of knowledge for future assimilation and use). As with all other higher-order animals, however, proper behavior may be obtained through training.[17] After four million years of tribal living, it is safe to assume that mankind is tribal by instinct and therefore not inclined intellectually or genetically to practice diversity in any form related to survival. Is it unnatural for us to be diverse or at least accept diversity? I believe it is because humans are instinctive animals that have developed intelligence, not intelligent beings that are instinctive. For millions of years, taking care of oneself and one's closest relatives has been essential to human survival, and yet we have been asked for the last 5,776 years (by the Hebrew calendar), out of 4 million years, to change—beginning with God's commanding us to love our neighbors as much as we love ourselves. Early man put it another way: eat thy neighbor.

Many religions, from earliest times, declare diversity as a mandate, but the historical definition of diversity was much different. In Judaism, all men were considered sons of the same father, which implied that they were equal in the covenant of the people with God. The monotheistic creed of the Jewish people is epitomized in the idea of one God, *father* of all men. Buddhism teaches *men* respect for life and the condemnation of violence. Chinese civilization exalts civic responsibility and altruism and elaborates upon the duties of citizens as well as the duties of *man*. Rene Cassin, writes in From the Ten Commandments to the Rights of Man, that the Greeks believed freedom should be restricted to certain citizens only, and Aristotle, the one-man think tank, considered the distinction between *free men* and those doomed by nature to slavery to be self-evident. Christianity is first and foremost a religion of redemption. Aside from gaining redemption through the gift of grace for the soul, Christians believe in living lives of loving their *fellow men* and themselves. Far from mentioning the rights of the individual, the sole concern is to prepare on earth for a good death.

RELIGION AND DIVERSITY

Religion must be considered when building a more diverse workforce. For much of our society and in certain geographic regions it is a powerful influence and we must recognize how one reconciles religious diversity with business, education, income, political orientation and belief in science, all potential elements in building a corporate culture.

This is an area where diversity for diversity's sake can have a negative effect on a business. How does one fit the following into a work environment?

* Muslims observe five formal prayers each day. The timings of these prayers are spaced evenly throughout the day so that one is constantly reminded of God and given opportunities to seek his guidance and forgiveness.
* Observant Jews pray three time a day. They do not work from Friday sundown to Saturday sundown, and there are many other holidays and fast days when work is prohibited.
* Christians, depending on their religiosity, have many holy days and periods: Lent, Palm Sunday, Maundy Thursday, Good Friday, Easter, Pentecost, Advent, and Christmas. Additionally, depending on one's denomination, there can be many more days and periods to observe.
* Asia was the birthplace of many religions, such as Hinduism, Buddhism, Confucianism, Taoism, Jainism, Sikhism, and Zoroastrianism, as well as many other religions, and Asians are migrating to the United States in record numbers.

How does a business adapt to atheists, agnostics and other non-believers? The rituals, if any, of these different institutions should accommodate the business and at the same time adhere to Title VII of the Civil Rights Act of 1964 that requires employers to "reasonably accommodate employees' sincerely held religious beliefs, observances and practices when requested, unless accommodation would impose an undue hardship on business operations." This means accommodation and consideration for employees of various religions, be it allowing employees to decorate their personal spaces, scheduling to accommodate employees' religious practices, supplying foods that meet various religion-based dietary needs, modifying the dress code, providing designated space for religious practices, providing paid leave for holidays, or allowing on-site religion-based affinity groups to meet.[18]

It is doubtful that building a diverse workforce would incorporate all the above-mentioned religions and practices but a company must be prepared to do so with not only their employees but an ever expanding, diverse and global consumer. Traditionally, diversity was not part of religious studies, nor was it a requirement of salvation in Christianity. It has been accepted and expected only in the last fifty years. According to Ian S. Markham in *The Oxford Handbook of Religious Diversity*, the emergence of religious studies as a discipline was part of a quest to approach religious diversity in a way that ensures that we explore "the other" in a way that does not misrepresent it. Is it any wonder that trainers, or those designated to teach and support diversity in the workplace, have such difficulty explaining a subject so vast and contradictory? Trainers are mostly following scripts created for them to ensure they are following the law—and they are protected from those same laws. Many trainers do not have a degree of comfort relative to the subject matter for specific company concerns for the trainees to feel the confidence to communicate their importance effectively.

DIVERSITY CONTINUES TO BE A TOUGH SELL. HERE'S WHY:

The government encourages it, but in most cases, this is not a positive, since it causes resentment on both sides. No one likes the government telling them what to do.

* Political parties are more exclusionary than ever and in some cases downright mean spirited.
* Social exclusion relates to the alienation or disenfranchisement of certain people within a society based on many factors, including income and profession. Those entities that traditionally exclude certain people include clubs, resorts, condos, co-ops, schools, and so on.
* Communities may self-exclude by removing themselves physically from the larger community. For example, in the gated-community model, the gate is intended to provide a physical block to outsiders, but symbolically it means that unless you belong, stay out
* Are Koreatown, Chinatown, Little Italy, Harlem, Greektown, Little India, Williamsburg (Brooklyn), Irishtown, Little Tokyo, Little Saigon, Filipinotown, Little Pakistan, Little Portugal, and all the other ethnic enclaves around the United States discriminatory or welcoming districts of hospitality? Do they intend to keep others out or provide a comfortable haven that looks and feels in some way like home for those who desire traditional surroundings?

Understanding diversity is not easy. Diversity doesn't mean holding hands and singing songs in the conference room over takeout sandwiches. It doesn't mean featuring minorities prominently in annual reports to show shareholders and the world that the company embraces everyone. It does means giving everyone a good reason to accept diversity and understand that there are far-reaching benefits that have nothing to do with quotas or annual report pictures.

Some questions that everyone who is working in a company diversity program should ask are as follows:

* Does diversity do anything to help employees be more successful?
* Does diversity improve profitability?
* Is the company diverse in all departments, positions, and compensation?
* Does the training work and should it be mandatory?
* Should the company be diverse in all departments, positions, and compensation?
* Should the company be a standard-bearer for diversity?
* Does the CEO really believe in diversity, or is it just a box on a checklist? (The CEO position is the least diverse in corporate America, which tells you all you really need to know.)

Here are some of the top companies rated by diversity experts and organizations:

WAL-MART (#1 ON FORBES 100)

* Hispanic Business Diversity Elite winner
* Top Companies for Executive Women: National Association for Female Executives

* Best Companies for Asian-Pacific Americans: *Asian Enterprise* magazine
* Top Diversity Employers for African-Americans: *Black EOE Journal*
* Best Supplier Diversity Programs for Hispanics: *Hispanic Network* magazine
* Top 50 Employers: Equal Opportunity Publications
* Top 50 Companies for Disabled People: *Careers & the Disabled* magazine
* 20 Best Companies for Diverse Graduates: *Diversity Edge* magazine
* Top 20 Best Companies for Multicultural Women: Working Mother Media
* LATINA Style 50 Companies: *LatinaStyle* magazine
* Corporation of the Year Award: National Asian-Pacific Council on Aging
* Top 50 Companies for Diverse Managers to Work: *Diversity MBA* magazine[20]
* Board of directors: fifteen members, of whom twelve are male, three are female, one is Hispanic, and two are African-American
* Wal-Mart Company blurb: *"Diversity is a way of life at Wal-Mart and our commitment to diversity is not just something we talk about, it's who we are. Our dedication to diversity extends from our board of directors, to our associates; from our suppliers, to our customers; and to every aspect of our business. We have long maintained diversity initiatives, including personnel practices and supplier programs, to help build and retain a diverse workforce and supplier base along with varied community outreach programs."*[21]

BANK OF AMERICA (#26 ON FORBES 100)

* Hispanic Business Diversity Elite winner
* Top 50 Companies for Diversity, no. 3: *DiversityInc* magazine
* Best 100 Companies: *Working Mother* magazine:
* National Association for the Advancement of Colored People (NAACP)'s Economic Reciprocity Initiative Report cited B of A for opportunity and fairness
* Top 50 Companies: *LatinaStyle* magazine
* 100 percent Corporate Equality Index: Human Rights Campaign (third consecutive year)
* Executive committee: thirteen members, of whom ten are male, three are female, and one is African American
* Company blurb: *"We respect and value not only differences related to race, gender, ethnicity, disability, and sexual orientation, but also diversity of viewpoint, experience, talents, and ideas. We strive to empower all associates to excel on the job and reach their full potential."*[22]

APPLE #3

* *"Diversity is more than any one gender, race, or ethnicity. It's richly representative of all people, all backgrounds, and all perspectives. It is the entire human experience.* "reports Apples CEO Tim Cook.
  Apple Diversity Organizations: [23]
    o African American Employee Association
    o Agnostic Community at Apple
    o Amigos@Apple
    o Apple Asian Association
    o Apple Christian Fellowship
    o Apple Indian Association

- Apple Jewish Association
  - Apple Muslim Association
  - Pride@Apple
  - Women@Apple
* Apple states that it has increased the percentage of female new hires from 31% in 2014 to 37% so far in 2016
* 100% score on HRC's (Human Rights Campaign) Corporate Equality Index for 13th year running
* Apple committed over $40 million to the Thurgood Marshall College Fund, which will use the money to create a database of computer science majors at HBCUs (historically black colleges and universities)
* Apple partnered with, the National Center for Women and Information Technology (NCWIT), to help create a broader pipeline of female technology workers. —giving about $10 million.
* 2015 Readers' Choice Award #6 – *Workforce Diversity*- positive working environment for members of minority groups
* Of eight people on Apple's Board, two are women, one is a Black male and five are white male.
* Apple's executive team is overwhelming white and male. Out of 18 positions three are women – two of whom are black. The other 15 are filled by white men.
* Apple, in its proxy stated, "Apple has demonstrated to shareholders its commitment to inclusion and diversity, which are core values for our company." CEO Tim Cook noted, "we know there is a lot more work to be done".

Here's a handy list of what diversity should do for business but hasn't really done yet. Read on to find out how to make it happen and make it stick:

* Diversity should unite associates with various backgrounds and knowledges to form a more innovative and productive group. Experience has determined that drawing on diverse group will strengthen the bottom line. Diversity is an important ingredient in building a strong and inclusive company that's created to last.
* Diversity is necessary for a successful business; it boosts creativity, creativity and enterprise, diversity gives a business a competitive advantage.
* Diversity is an opportunity. A diverse workforce can be more innovative due to their uniqueness, varied experiences and viewpoints. This makes a company more sustainable.
* Diversity is a priority. Understanding that investing in a diverse workforce allows the know-how to stay ahead of the shift to globalization while protecting the company at home.
* Diversity can be a secret weapon. To drive growth in new markets a company must build tolerance, have bilingual associates and form partnerships around the world. By diversifying the workforce, a company can gain more market share by better understanding diverse customers.
* Diversity is an advantage; Companies must develop an understanding of other cultural knowledge to successfully participate with those who represent a changing marketplace
* Diversity adds to the bottom line; by increasing market share which a diverse workforce is proven to do, company sells more product hence increasing the return on investment. Studies have shown that a diverse workforce decreases employee turnover which reduces costs which positively affects the bottom line.

Diversity is about leadership. It is essential to have a Strategic Plan for Diversity and that must come from the top. Diversity must be seen by all as a key element to the success of the company and that must be driven down the organization by leadership. Diversity must be built into the culture of the business and the CEO is responsible for the culture of the business. Having a leader who is visible and displays the intensity required by the organization leads to an effective program.

Chapter 3

TIMES ARE CHANGING

Happy days are here again!
The skies above are clear again,
Let us sing a song of cheer again,
Happy days are here again!

So long sad times, go long bad times,
We are rid of you at last;
Howdy gay times, cloudy gray times
You are now a thing of the past.
Happy days are here again!

Times have changed. No longer can businesses selling a product or products connect with their customers using an all-purpose marketing strategy. The consumer marketplace has changed and continues to evolve as the population grows more and more dissimilar, what we now label as minority groups, together, will make up the majority of the population by 2040. According to the US Census Bureau, in 2014 there were more than twenty million children under five years old living in the United States, and 50.2

percent of them were minorities.[24] Not only is the population different, but how one looks at the populace can be confusing, as "some people are both, majority and minority."[25]

The minority population is defined as any group that is not in the majority normally used in racial, ethnic, and religious terms, is expected to rise to 56 percent of the total population in 2050, compared with 38 percent in 2015. When that happens, "no group will have a majority share of the total and the United States will become a 'plurality' of racial and ethnic groups," according to the US Census Bureau.[26] The minority-majority trend reflected among five-year-olds is the beginning of this shift. For children, diversity needs to be real and not merely relegated to learning the names of a few prominent African Americans during Black History Month or enjoying south-of-the-border cuisine on Cinco de Mayo. It means talking to and spending time with kids "not like them" so that they may discover those kids are in fact just like them.[27]

ETHNIC GROUPS
WHITE AMERICANS

The majority of the more than 320 million people currently living in the United States are white Americans, who trace their ancestry to the original peoples of Europe, the Middle East, and North Africa. White Americans are the majority in forty-nine of the fifty states, with Hawaii as the lone exception. The non-Hispanic white percentage, 63 percent in 2013, an all-time low, tends to decrease every year. This subgroup is expected to be reduced to a plurality of the overall US population by the year 2050. The Census Bureau reports that 50.5 million (16.3 percent) Americans identify as Hispanic or Latino. Of those, 267 million (53 percent) also identify as white. Whites (including Hispanics who identify as white) constitute the majority, with a total of about 247 million, or 77.35 percent of the population as of 2014. Non-Hispanic whites totaled about 198 million, or 62.06 percent of the US population.[28]

In shaping workplaces, one can no longer simply think of black and white or Christian and non-Christian. Although there are strong conflicts between blacks and whites, nearly two-thirds of blacks say there are significant conflicts between the rich and poor, and 61 percent say there are significant conflicts between immigrants and the native born. Blacks also are twice as likely as whites to see major generational conflicts.[29] Regardless of race, a study by the Pew Research Center reports that the deepest social conflicts occur between immigrants and the native born. These same conflicts and divides carry over into the workplace and politics, instigating partisan and ideological differences together with racial, generational, and ethnic divides. The workplace has become more difficult to manage productively and requires management skills that were not even defined twenty years ago. It is a more difficult assignment reaching out to the customers of these companies in an effective and comprehensible style.

BLACK OR AFRICAN-AMERICANS

About 12.4 percent of the American people are black or African American. Known more simply as black Americans, the black American group is the largest racial minority, as compared to Hispanics and Latinos, who are the largest *ethnic* minority. Historically, all people with any sub-Saharan African ancestry, even if they were mostly white, were designated and classified as black.[30] This was known as the "one-drop" (of blood) rule and was meant to ensure a child of mixed heritage would be assigned to the group with the lower status. Although one-drop laws no longer exist, the concept remains somewhat ubiquitous, and it is used by people of European backgrounds, belying the theory that we will one day be race neutral, which is impossible

ASIAN AMERICANS

A third significant minority is the Asian American population, comprising 13.4 million (4.4 percent) of the US population in 2008. California is home to 4.5 million Asian Americans, whereas 495,000 live in Hawaii, where they compose the plurality of the island's people, the largest share of any state. Asians are by no means a monolithic group. There is no Asian race; they are multiracial. The largest subgroups are immigrants or descendants of immigrants from the Philippines, China, India, Brunei, Malaysia, Vietnam, Cambodia, Taiwan, South Korea, Japan, and Thailand. Most Americans do not understand the differences between Asian cultures of specific countries, biracial Asians, and multiracial Asians, a marketing problem that impedes marketing efforts to this key demographic. If a company doesn't understand the underlying markets, its plan will be destined to fail, as diversity marketing signifies that there is not a "one ad fits all" when it comes to marketing to the various Asian communities

HISPANIC AND LATINO AMERICANS

"Hispanic or Latino origin" is a self-designation made by forty-seven million Americans as of 2008. They have origins in the Spanish-speaking nations of Latin America, chiefly, whereas a small percentage traces its origins to Spain. The Hispanic or Latino population is young and fast growing, owing to immigration and higher birth rates. For decades, it has contributed significantly to US population increases, and this is expected to continue for decades. The Census Bureau projects that by 2050 one-quarter of the population will be Hispanic or Latino.[31]

HOW TO ACCOMPLISH MULTI-CULTURAL MARKETING

Consumers in various cultures have different values, experiences, expectations, and ways of interacting. Even within a culture, such differences are apparent between various subgroups, based not just on ethnicity but also on age, suggesting that marketing and advertising must offer alternative ways of communicating to consumers in each of the groups. The future of America's "melting pot" has been at the center of political debate regarding topics such as immigration, schools, jobs, wages, and religion. Conservatives believe that large-scale immigration is dangerous both to our nation's security and to its social and moral fabric. At the same time, politically correct progressives may deny the reality of the challenge that social solidarity poses to diversity. The recipe has changed, and the ingredients now required for the melting pot have changed. In the past limited talent for factory jobs were required and manual labor, construction, and trade opportunities were readily available and could be mastered by most immigrants. To succeed today, we need to do a better job recruiting immigrants, and that means we had better know how to market jobs and the United States to individuals with the skill sets that are considered necessary. A diversified workforce and workplace might require distinct skills, a specific language, and various backgrounds. The most successful customer service business in the world states; "*Amazon has hundreds of millions of customers who can benefit from diversity of thought. We are a company of builders who bring varying backgrounds, ideas, and points of view to inventing on behalf of our customers. Our diverse perspectives come from many sources including gender, race, age, national origin, sexual orientation, disability, culture, education, as well as professional and life experience. We are working to develop leaders and shape future talent pools to help us meet the needs of our customers around the world. As we invest in global programs to accelerate our progress, we want to share some of our actions".*[32]

In a thirty-thousand-subject study in forty-one US communities, Harvard political scientist Robert Putnam found that the greater the diversity in a community and the less homogenous it is, the less neighbors trust one another, the less people vote and volunteer, and the less they give to charity and work on community projects. The politically correct message has always been the same: the more diverse the parts, the stronger the whole. But the reality differs. The study is part of a fascinating new portrait of diversity emerging from recent scholarship. Diversity, it shows, makes us uncomfortable.[33]

Diversity for Fun and Profit hypothesizes that diversity may not be natural or comfortable, and yet to succeed in an ever-changing society, businesses must understand these various cultures and races to produce the products these customers want and have the right message to express the offer.

Although I have used scholarly research and cite academia to both support and at times challenge many customary principles and opinions concerning diversity that are recognized by both the academic and professional diversity world, I do not believe businesses can effectively build a workforce using these somewhat outdated methods of training to reach the customer they are targeting. *Diversity for Fun and Profit* offers a proven formula that demonstrates a methodology to build an organization and acquire the necessary resources for the development and sales of products to what I oxymoronically label the "homogeneously diverse" customer, or a diverse but tight-knit group of customers, not actually diverse at all. It is a difficult assignment to build a homogeneously diverse organization. When done successfully, the rewards are significant to the bottom line, but if some employees may appear different from their peers, subordinates, and managers they are "homogeneous to the customer and will have better insights into their needs. At the same time, a homogeneous group that matches the consumer must be present in the organization to ensure the basics are always covered. This is the opposite of diversity as usually defined.

Here is an example of when not understanding the customer was very costly to one American company, a company where I was the CEO. The company had been successful with a national chain of fashion stores targeting middle-income black women and a second division of Latina stores located in Puerto Rico, Florida and the Caribbean. Due to the success of the Latina stores an assumption was made that we "couldn't miss" targeting the large Hispanic population in California, Texas, and the Southwest, and management was directed to test a new concept. Unlike either the black-centric business or the Latina, which was managed predominantly by customer-centric associates, the new division did not have any Mexican American merchants or management and failed to do proper due diligence. Management proceeded with a prototype store design, real estate, and merchandise at a price bought for its interpretation of the customer. Although several national and regional chains were doing business in these same areas with merchandise and store design identical to stores merchandised to non-Hispanic customers the board and we as management believed that Hispanic women would flock to these stores designed just for them. Like the African-American stores and those in the Caribbean we believed the Hispanic customer would welcome and be appreciative of a store of their own designed just for them. Five Hispanic stores were opened, all with great real estate, Spanish-speaking staff, marketing materials in Spanish, and music and entertainment at the grand opening. None of the stores was profitable. We were puzzled, was it the merchandise, service, or store design? How could these beautiful stores be failing? Finally, but too late, management held focus groups to see what they could learn, and learn they did. "Why do you think we want our own stores?" focus group members from the Hispanic market said. "We are Americans just like everyone else. We have been here many years. We are not illegals. We are American." The success with black customers was due to great product which this customer required in addition to and an understanding of the prejudice those customers faced in most stores, better known as "shopping while black," which our African American–led management team understood. They made sure everything in those stores was perfect for that customer. The Hispanic customer did not have those barriers and instead believed the company thought they were second class citizens. There was no going back, no way to redeem the stores; no self-respecting Hispanic was going to shop in there, the community made sure of that, and soon the stores closed. This company later learned there is a Hispanic market, just as there is one for Poles, Russians, Italians, and Jews, but these are markets related to customs, food, religion, and restaurants, not clothing or product available anywhere. And we, the so-called experts on multicultural marketing, had no Mexican American merchants or marketers. Though we understood the differences between Latino and Hispanic, and knew Caribbean and Mexican cultures were very different, we never thought anyone would be downright insulted by the stores.

So long sad times, go long bad times,
We are rid of you at last;
Howdy gay times, cloudy gray times
You are now a thing of the past.
The skies above are clear again
Happy days are here again!

GENDER DIVERSITY

Are women a defined minority or just discriminated against? The number of females in the United States as of July 2015, was 162 million, and the number of males was 157 million. The number of females sixteen and older who participated in the civilian labor force in 2015 was 75.6 million, or 47.4 percent of the civilian labor force.[34] Among women twenty-five and older, 30.7 million have a bachelor's degree, higher than the corresponding number for men (29.2 million). Women have a larger share of high school diplomas (including equivalents), as well as associate's, bachelor's, and master's degrees. Additional census data shows that 71.9 million women, or 58.6 percent of the female workforce sixteen and older, participate in the labor force, and 40.6 percent of females sixteen and older work in management, professional, and related occupations, compared with 34.2 percent of employed males. Yet women working full time in the United States typically are paid just 79 percent of what men are paid, a gap of 21 percent. Not only is there a national pay gap, but the gap varies from state to state. Per data from the American Community Survey, in 2015 the pay gap was smallest in Washington, DC, where women were paid 90 percent of what men were paid, and largest in Louisiana, where women were paid 65 percent of what men were paid.[35]

To add to the confusion—or is it a deliberate strategy? — Hispanic, African American, American Indian, and Native Hawaiian women have lower median annual earnings compared with non-Hispanic white and Asian American women. But within racial/ethnic groups, African American, Hispanic, American Indian, and Native Hawaiian women experience a smaller gender pay gap compared with men in the same group than do non-Hispanic white and Asian American women.[35] The gap is largest for Hispanic and Latina women, who were paid only 54 percent of what white men were paid in 2015. Pay equity may be affected by the segregation of jobs by gender and other factors. The Institute for Women's Policy Research (IWPR) shows that "irrespective of the level of qualification, jobs predominantly done by women pay less on average than jobs predominantly done by men." [36]

According to a recent regression analysis of federal data by IWPR, the poverty rate for working women would be cut in half if women were paid the same as comparable men. Based on today's wage gap, a woman who worked full time, year-round, would typically lose $430,480 in a forty-year period.[37] This woman would have to work nearly eleven years longer to make up this lifetime wage gap. A woman working full time, year-round, who started but did not finish high school would typically lose $354,080 over a forty-year period compared to her male counterpart. This is an enormous amount of money for women who typically make $21,986 a year. A woman would have to work sixteen years longer to make up this gap. These lost wages severely reduce women's ability to save for retirement. Because of lower lifetime earnings and different work patterns, the average social security benefit for women sixty-five and older is about $13,867 per year, compared to $18,039 for men of the same age.[38] In looking at discrimination based on gender, women are not a statistical minority—in most societies, they are roughly equal in number to men—but they do qualify as a minority group because they tend to have less power and fewer privileges than men. Although women have made strides in gaining access to education and employment, to this day they continue to face significant hurdles that men generally do not confront. Although there has been improvement, women have always been treated like second-class citizens in the US workforce.

When discussing and designing a program for gender diversity, it is important to have men, women and LGBTQ associates involved in the planning. Even with the best of planning I have found that these gender programs are not enough and old behaviors often return if they are not practiced every day and if leadership does not set the example. Writing a plan is not enough; the key to success is having the enthusiasm and discipline to implement it.

Chapter 4

WE CAN'T FIND ANY OF THOSE

In 1991, I was recruited as the president of a retail business headquartered in upstate South Carolina. It was an off-price retail women's fashion business comprising about 250 stores, most located in small rural communities. The business had been on a downturn for two years after early success that included a successful public offering. Everything in the store was either one low price or a multiple of that price. So, if a top was marked seven dollars, the matching bottom was also seven dollars, making the outfit fourteen dollars. Accessories might be priced at three for seven dollars, T-shirts two for seven dollars, and so on. Most of the merchandise was branded and bought in the off-price garment market. Everything was first quality, no damages or irregulars and was an exceptional value. It was a terrific concept and allowed the customer to get a bargain on clothing that was priced at least double in other stores. I was brought in to "fix" the business and restore it to profitability and restart its growth. After several months of visiting stores and assessing the company, I realized the problem; the stores were all in small towns where there simply were not enough customers to sustain the desired growth. When a store initially opened, there was the "restaurant effect." Everyone near and far came to see this one-price store, which resulted in extremely strong openings. But as with restaurants, whence the name of the effect originates, these initial sales were not sustainable, and the sales leveled off. The company's locations in these small towns predetermined limited sales that could not grow proportionately and the business became stagnant. Since the solution to fix the stores was either attracting more customers or raising prices I concluded the business model was flawed, and a new model had to be found. In my analysis, I determined that the fundamentals were sound: great product, reasonable occupancy costs, and good logistics but based on an innovative strategic plan we developed, I realized we had to make major changes to the organization because of what we had learned. One of the main findings was the associates lacked the diversity of the customer mix and the stores were in under-sized markets and changes had to be made if the business was to be saved. Many customers were low income and, even in small towns, disproportionately composed of minorities. Here we were, with a workforce that did not match or understand the customer. I knew from experience in other companies and demographics that there were millions of customers who would appreciate our product, but most lived, worked and shopped in urban areas. I set out to test and verify my theory. Knowing this customer was more selective owing to a more competitive shopping environment, we needed to hire merchants and marketers who would understand this consumer and bring additional skills to the company. Very little of the retail expertise required was readily available in upstate South Carolina, therefore we recruited an HR executive who had the knowhow to recruit people with merchandising and marketing skills. Additionally, we hired a lead real estate manager experienced in working in urban markets. Our goal was to be sure we were not only price right but also fashion right, as this customer understood style and had aspirational needs many of our veteran buyers and marketers didn't understand. I was in the Deep South, managing a business composed primarily of white men. We began our recruiting campaign at companies where we believed our prospective customers shopped. Convincing minorities to come south to a retailer with a concept that seemed foreign to them was not as difficult as I thought. We offered opportunity and leadership roles, whereas their current employers, like many companies, did not extend them these opportunities. In six months, we managed to recruit several merchants, a lead merchandise planner, new marketing personnel, and several store directors who understood—and in many cases, were part of—the community we wanted to serve.

But there was a hitch or two; I will always remember the day I started making calls to friends in the business and telling them the wonders of the New South and all the opportunities that would be. available to them. That same night a story broke on all the major news shows and in newspapers, including the *New York Times* and metropolitan—New York, the garment center of the country, was where most of my recruits lived or worked. The story detailed that students at the high school in Duncan, South Carolina—the small town where our offices and distribution center were located—were protesting the school's policy that the Confederate flag not be worn or displayed on school property. The story was everywhere. As I was raving about the home prices, culture, and opportunity, the Rebels (the sport team's name) continued their protest for free speech and their heritage. Over the weekend, many outsiders, including a handful of skinheads from North Carolina, joined the protest. Oh, swell. What could be worse? How about the planned opening of a Ku Klux Klan museum and another national story that lasted for several weeks?

Somehow, we got past the problems and were successful in bringing in some top talent. As would be expected, there was much skepticism in the ranks and on the board, but we moved ahead with the first two urban stores one in Brooklyn and another in Chicago. The stores in the small markets averaged sales of under $375,000 per year. The Brooklyn and Chicago stores opened at annual rates of $2 million each. We had found our new concept and would soon open in Detroit, Washington, Baltimore, New Orleans, and Philadelphia.

Over the next five years, we closed most of the rural stores and opened over four hundred urban locations. In 1999, the Chicago MSA (metropolitan statistical area) was the third largest MSA by population in the United States, with a population of 8,181,939. For comparison, the population of the state of West Virginia was 1.8 million, and the company had three stores there with sales totaling $850,000. It was an easy decision to close those stores along with the other rural locations and transition the business to high-population areas with tens of thousands of customers in a one-mile radius. Moving into metropolitan areas brought us into less familiar cultural groups, which required associates who understood those communities and how to buy the right product for the customer and how to market to them. We realized we still had a long way to go one fashion season when purple was the hot color and we were selling everything we could get—except in certain areas of the newly opened Los Angeles market. After visiting the stores there and speaking with the associates and customers, we learned that in the Hispanic community, purple is a funeral color. Another lesson learned, and we soon put a team together to teach the business how to address this important demographic, which became one of the company's major contributors to profits as we opened in Texas and the border states.

Without building a workforce that would understand these consumers, the company would have failed. Instead, the stock price quadrupled and split over the next two years. Because this company offered opportunities to minorities, it could attract the talent needed. When people came to visit, they saw a diverse group of associates at all levels working together and dependent on one another for success. Never did the company feel compelled to hold a diversity meeting or call in diversity experts to discuss cultural sensitivity, empathy, or respect. The company had been rebuilt for corporate and individual success using practical methods, with diversity and inclusion integrated into the job descriptions and daily procedures of employees. I can't say everyone was successful in this corporate culture, but to be successful, one had to accept it.

How does a company build an organization that meets the requirements of the business? You begin by developing a strategic plan to identify and measure the core values of the business and its relevance to your marketplace. Matching an organization's goods and services with its markets should be based on an understanding of the company's mission, customers, associates, and offerings, whether formal or informal. To have no strategy is to be directionless. A multicultural, talented, and trained employee base gives a company an advantage, and that same diversity in expertise allows for a more balanced approach to marketing. A report on the economic imperative of managing diversity by Covenant Investment Management that includes more than seventy pages of analysis concluded simply: "Organizations which excel at leveraging diversity (including the hiring and advancement of women and non-white men into senior management jobs, and providing a climate conducive to contributions from people of diverse backgrounds) will experience better financial performance in the long run than organizations which are not effective in managing diversity."[39] The bottom line "is that diversity is profitable," especially in a society that by the year 2050 will be evenly split between whites and non-whites, as quoted a report, *Competitiveness through Management of Diversity: Effects on Stock Price Valuation*.[40] Business lags the population; minorities are the majority in six of the eight largest metropolitan areas of the United States, yet few companies are minority owned or managed. Women are the primary investors in more than half of US households and are responsible for well over 55 percent of the buying power in the United States, yet they hold only 4 percent of the positions of CEO at Fortune 500 companies. Latinos hold only 2 percent of CEO jobs, and African Americans only 1.2 percent. The combined black, Hispanic, and Asian buying power is more than $750 billion annually. Market estimates vary, but women have a total purchasing power ranging anywhere from $5 trillion to $15 trillion annually.[40] Considering the spending power that women and minorities have, it is imperative for customer communications to resonate with them. Specifically, Nielsen Research has found that the female brain is hardwired with evolutionary strongholds to create a very specialized customer whose purchasing prowess has never been stronger.[41] Retention is an important step toward loyalty. I have found that women's loyalty to a company in both is greater than men's and women, in my opinion, tend to better understand many industries including women's fashion. Since women control America's purse strings, it would seem logical for women to be employed in many of the positions that relate to other women. To successfully compete in today's and tomorrow's marketplace, companies' must identify with their customers and understand and recruit a workforce able to compete in a diverse global market. And while diverse organizations continue to grow at the lower levels, senior and upper management—as well as the boardroom—remains male dominated. It isn't because qualified individuals are not available; it is because those responsible for hiring are not comfortable hiring minorities. And they are not comfortable owing to fear and prejudice, since they were never exposed to the training and populaces required. Once managers realize they will be more successful in their jobs and are rewarded appropriately, diversity will begin to take hold in the company.

When I was the CEO of Urban Brands, which owned the Ashley Stewart Stores and Marianne Puerto Rico, we had a rule that no visitor was to wait in the lobby more than fifteen minutes and if someone was kept waiting the front desk was to call me and I would escort the person to their appointment. The point was that if the CEO could take the time to meet and greet, then the associate who had kept the visitor waiting should realize how important this courtesy was to the culture of the company. One afternoon the front desk called me and reported that a candidate was in the lobby for an interview and the fifteen-minute time limit was up. I went to pick up the candidate but no one was there and the desk associate told me he had just walked out. I thought this was odd as he had had several previous interviews off our premises and seemed excited about the company. I assumed he left due to the wait but decided to follow-up with a phone call to better understand what had happened and in doing so learned a valuable lesson about diversity. While sitting in our lobby the candidate observed dozens of our associates walking through the lobby going about their business. We had a workforce that was 97% people of color and 98% women and the candidate, a white male, felt he would be uncomfortable being a minority. It was a revelation to me as I was so used to being one of the only white males in the room that I never thought I was different or would have a problem fitting in. Now, I do understand being the boss placed me in a different position than the candidate but I had to consider perhaps we were not as diverse as I had thought. I had built the organization from a predominately white male environment to a workplace population that matched the customer, African American and Latino women. Were we missing out on talent we needed and was this an issue that affected others looking in? We had won several national awards that year for workplace diversity but we were not essentially very diverse. We were right in understanding the needs of our customers and we knew how to reach her, and a traditional EEOC workshop program would probably not work for this business but, were we doing enough to ensure that the minority associates, men and whites, understood the customer and were comfortable in our environment. That was the "aha moment!" that led me to design "diversity" programs that match a company's purpose and how it defines itself and its customers. That process, discussed in this book, involves the development and design of a strategic diversity plan that will positively affect marketing campaigns for certain groups or demographics. *Diversity for Fun and Profit* explains to companies that customers have distinctive behaviors in addition to sex, age and race and clarifies how to best communicate to them to ensure and verify marketing success. It also forces the company to justify the need for a diversity plan in both human and economic capital.

Chapter 5

WHY CREATE A DIVERSE WORKPLACE

Song: Just as Well As He[41]
Music: to the tune of "Coming through the Rye"

If a body pays the taxes,
Surely, you'll agree That a body earns the franchise
Whether he or she...
Every man now has the ballot;
None you know have we,
But we have brains and we can use them
Just as well as he.

If a home that has a father
Needs a mother too,
Then every state has men voters
Needs its women too.

What is a minority group? Contemporary sociologists generally define a minority as a group of people differentiated from others in the same society by race, nationality, religion, or language, who both think of themselves as a differentiated group and are thought of by others as a differentiated group with negative connotations. The important elements in this definition are a set of attitudes—those of group identification from within the group and those of prejudice from without—and a set of behaviors—those of self- segregation from within the group and those of discrimination and exclusion from without.[42] All citizens of the United States share a common nationality, American. Therefore, based on nationality, all belong to the majority group, as it is the majority in the country. There are no other groups in the United States that form or even come close to the majority. There are those of us who believe the word "minority" has a pejorative connotation and aids in adding prejudice and negativity in discussions. In marketing, the belief is that labeling any customer in a negative fashion will have an adverse effect. We do define certain groups as minorities, although they may and probably are members of the majority. There are racial minorities, though few if any do not have a mix of races in their DNA.; nationality group minorities, minorities based on immigration or familial country of origin; language minorities, who, though they have other cultural traits, choose to speak the language of their origin and religious minorities. The position of the Jewish people is unlike that of other religious minorities because there are more people of Jewish descent than there are active believers in the Jewish religion. Indeed, it is likely that in the United States, believers and nonbelievers are about equal in number, although most of the latter would undoubtedly regard themselves as Jewish nonetheless.[43] Women are not a statistical minority, as in most societies—they are roughly equal in number to men—but they qualify as a minority group because they tend to have less power and fewer privileges than men. Underlying this unequal treatment of women is sexism, which is discrimination based on gender. Discrimination against women is obvious in many ways, whether political, legal, economic, or familial. Women, cannot seem to completely shake their role of second class citizens. You need to look no further than the inability to ratify the Equal Rights Amendment (ERA) to the Constitution giving the same rights to women as men. Gender inequality continues to be a problem in many companies affecting productivity and profits by excluding a key resource from the ranks of decision makers.

Many ethnic niches have unique needs and, in relation to other market segments, require effective communications to these diverse groups. There are many fundamental cultural aspects that sway behaviors and stimulate the desire to buy. A lack of knowledge can inhibit effective communication across cultures. It is imperative to have a cultural understanding of targeted groups to keep communication in the context of the target audience, and the best way to ensure that happens is to have those cultures represented in the workforce.

STUDY: MISCOMMUNICATING

Following the shooting and deaths of five police officers in Dallas in July 2016, former mayor Rudolph W. Giuliani of New York demonstrated exactly how not to communicate to minorities. Although there was not a product involved, a marketing plan was required to keep everyone on the same page and for the police and local government to, accomplish their goal of bettering community relations and policing. Demonstrating a lack of understanding of the black community, the former mayor, appearing on multiple talk shows and interviewed by members of the media, showed a lack of knowledge for the community sentiment and accused the Black Lives Matters group of ignoring black-on-black crime, inspiring violence against the police, and promoting racism. The former mayor displayed his ignorance —unlike other, more aware leaders whose messages of hope, unity, and understanding demonstrated what the correct message for both sides should be. Instead of advocating open channels of communication between the communities and the police to aid in understanding both viewpoints, the white mayor, with very little time spent in the Black neighborhoods as mayor of New York City and lacking comprehension of minorities, lectured the African American community on subjects which had nothing to do with the root of the current situations. William J. Bratton, the New York police commissioner at the time and the inventor of community policing, emphasized unity, saying, "This is a shared responsibility, trying to bridge these differences that are becoming quite evident."[44] Giuliani made matters worse by not having advisors around him who understood what the problems in the community were and addressing them. This is a direct correlation to not effectively communicating and losing credibility with the target audience.

Most white people do not understand the oppressive power of language "Many people use the word *minority* when they really mean African American, Jewish, Gay, Hispanic.[45] That is inaccurate, as it connotes they are subordinate to a dominant group." With most this country made up of minorities, understanding these individual groups, without prejudice and racism, is vital to understanding other's cultural backgrounds to avoid culture clashes.[46]

An example of an extreme lack of diversity and perhaps not understanding the importance of minorities in our society is the 2017 Presidential Cabinet consisting of 3 women and 17 men. The Cabinet is comprised of one African American, one Hispanic and two Asians. In my opinion, this is an organization with the probability of failure because of not having diverse points of view. In this group minorities and women have a greater chance of being overlooked because decision-making in a Cabinet as homogeneous as this could lack the needed probing assessments and be disastrously surprised due to a lack of divergent ideas and planning. It appears our White House might need a plan as it apparently does not understand diversity, as Sean Spicer, the White House Press Secretary, defended then President-elect Donald Trump's commitment to diversity, saying at that time "that the fact that the Cabinet will be the first in 30 years without a Latino is "a very narrow way to look at it." "The No. 1 thing that I think Americans should focus on is, 'Is he hiring the best and the brightest? Is he hiring people that are committed to enacting real change?'" I think that when you look at the totality at his administration — the people that he's talked to, the people that he's met with, the people that he's appointing — you see a president who's committed to uniting this country, who's bringing the best and brightest together," Spicer said. "Look at the cabinet — Elaine Chao, Dr. Ben Carson, Nikki Haley, the first Indian-American. [47]"

Almost all of Trump's cabinet is comprised of rich, white men. Out of the 15 formal slots, only two are people of color. Ben Carson, the secretary of Housing and Urban Development designate is African-American and Elaine Chao, the secretary of Transportation designate is Asian American.[47] The Cabinet does not match or compliment the citizens it is intended to represent.

BUILDING A DIVERSITY PLAN

Creating a diversity plan for your organization is key to ensuring that diversity and inclusion become integral to the way your business functions, both internally and externally. Several initial steps are necessary to guarantee that your group is prepared to create a diversity plan and understand its role within the community while addressing diversity in a meaningful and relevant way. Companies should avoid combining strategy reviews with discussions of budgets and financial targets, because when the two are considered together, short-term financial issues dominate at the expense of long-term strategic ones. There is a cost to diversity but it is minimal compared to many other investments in infrastructure. There is a cost to compliance but a benefit in lower legal costs and possible fines. There is a cost for education of staff but a benefit in retention, moral and direction. Some companies believe there is a diversion of management and staff time but studies show that diversity provides access to new markets; improved performance in existing markets; and better access to talent [48]

If you do not have the expertise in your organization, I recommend the CEO and a few key members of management attend an Executive Education Program at a Business Graduate School to learn how to design a program to build a solid foundation for your company's profitability and growth. I attended a program at UCLA's Anderson School of Management during my first tenure as a President and COO as I knew I hadn't developed the skills leaders need to achieve maximum impact on my organization. It is difficult to recognize your limitations but you must if you are to overcome them and to better understand the strategy necessary to drive results. Other options include consultants, AMA (American Management Association), software programs and templates. There is no substitute for leaders leading and understanding how the process works to provide the credibility required for the organization. It's the CEOs role to set direction and to send the message that he/she takes their direction-setting seriously.

If the company is large enough to have a Strategic Planning Officer or if a member of management has the mind-set, experience and knowledge of strategic planning it can be added to his/

her job description. The position contributes to the strategic planning, risk assessment and performance management activities of each department and the company. This individual works with the CEO and the associates in reviewing and updating planning documents, monitoring and measuring progress towards the company's goals and objectives; and regularly reports on results to the committee. Although there may be more, I consider the following six elements essential for a successful diversity plan.[49]

* A definition of diversity for the organization; The language used in diversity work is important and may vary. There are many interchangeable terms in defining diversity programming. To help your organization make the most of its diversity plan, make clear what your organization means by "diversity," and distinguish it from other terms.
* Your plan's definition should use specific examples and distinct explanations of what is included in the organization's concept of diversity. An assessment of need or justification for the diversity plan must be clearly identified
    o It should be straightforward in what diversity will contribute to the organization and the individuals within the organization. The business should define the requirements to be achieved by their proposal.
    o Leaders and managers must convey the plan to every part of the company. Leaders must lead by example and be completely committed.
    o The values, philosophy, resources, and commitment required for the organization's success must be spelled out, understood and communicated throughout the organization.
    o An assessment of need or justification for the diversity plan must be clearly identified

* Regular assessments must be scheduled to evaluate the plan's effectiveness and to evaluate whether the results are supporting the organizations objectives and goals.
  o Measurements should include:
    - Employee attrition rates
    - Employee satisfaction.
    - Market share within new customer bases
    - Awards and recognition
    - Enhancement of the culture of the organization
* A mission or vision for the diversity of the organization
  o The mission or vision statement for the diversity plan usually distills the organization's diversity definition and the environmental scan into a direct statement of how the company currently operates within the industry and what it strives to achieve and contribute as a diverse institution.
  o The mission and vision statement may restate the organization's definition of diversity and expand with several notes on the high-level strategies it will undertake to create or enhance a diverse environment.
* A statement of priorities or goals
  o An integral part of the diversity plan is the establishment of priorities and goals. Derived from the definition of diversity, priorities should articulate those areas where the plan hopes to see change within the organization
    - Awareness of diversity
    - Recruitment of diverse candidates
    - Communication and sharing among staff—and the goals and strategies that will be utilized. As is often suggested, goals should utilize a SMART approach—specific, measurable, attainable, realistic, and timely—and contribute to key priorities.

- The mission should always contain financial goals. "A good strategic plan includes metrics that translate the vision and mission into specific end points. This is critical because strategic planning is ultimately about resource allocation and would not be relevant if resources were unlimited."[50]
* A delegation of responsibilities toward achievement of the plan
  o Clearly articulate the plan's mission and goals
  o Clearly identify barriers and problems
  o Senior management should be responsible for various segments of the plan and they in turn should task associates depending on skill levels. Ensure associates are accountable to the assigned tasks
  o Large portions of the plan should be broken into smaller segments.
* A statement of accountability
  o In addition to measuring performance in each priority area based on the achievement of stated goals, the business can also utilize an activity grid to document specific activities that contribute to specific priorities and address specific customers or constituencies within the diversity plan.

BUILDING SUPPORT

When crafting a viable diversity plan, it is critical that buy-in exists at all levels of the company—from the board and CEO, the executive management, to the front-line staff. Buy-in across the organization is necessary for the plan to be viable and meaningful. Among the most important first steps in establishing cross organizational support is the alignment of an organization's strategic priorities with diversity. Consider exploring the corporate mission or vision statement to identify terms or clauses that can be connected back to issues of diversity: how increased organizational performance, enhanced customer use or satisfaction, or improved recruitment and retention can increase managers' desire to support diversity. As we will discuss later, including compelling, achievable, and beneficial goals in the diversity plan will help articulate the return on investment the business will receive.

PROCESS

The process of developing diversity plans has become much more inclusive. Businesses might invest up to a year or more in bringing together various individuals and groups—including not only management but also representative associates, users, clients, outside experts, customers, and community partners—to provide input into the preparing of recommendations. Diversity planning today is a much more bottom-up process and might involve meetings with a variety of constituencies both in and out of the business. These efforts result in better goals, a greater purpose of shared vision and mission, and a more focused and productive plan.

ASSESSING NEED—THE ENVIRONMENTAL SCAN (SWOT)

Diversity planning can vary depending on location, population, resources, and climate. It is helpful to review what similar businesses and institutions have developed, but it is also important to assess the internal climate of your organization and the external environment in which you exist. An environmental scan will help identify allies, gaps, and resource availability.

Assessing the diversity of your organization's internal environment is just as important as surveying the community in which your organization exists and the customer it serves. An internal scan can include many things, but among the most obvious are reviews of existing policies or statements (mission, vision, strategic plan) that address diversity; staff demographics; existing programs, activities, or collections that address diversity; and stakeholder or partner demographics. I have found that diversity promotes a more resourceful and inventive organization. Having associates with various experiences and life circumstances will assist in solving problems and providing solutions to thorny questions. Also, diversity generates creativity and innovation. In my businesses, I have always recruited diverse teams that I believe produced more innovative results than teams composed of associates with similar backgrounds.

The scan should include and define the following:

* Business trends
    o Identify what will drive success in the period being discussed in the plan- price vs value vs performance, sales, marketing strategy, recruiting and employee well-being and other key components of the business.
    o What are the technology needs and developments required now and in the future and are the personnel in place who understand and can fulfill these prerequisites?
* Product comparison
    o Be objective in rating competitive products
    o How does the consumer rate the products?
    o What is the brand recognition of comparative products?
    o What is the ease of buying the product?
    o Are there social, health, safety or environmental consequences of the various products?

- Test your products against the competitions
- What is the marketing strategy of the competition?
- How does the online representation compare and the ease of navigation on the sites?

* Demographic
  - A good way to gather consumer demographic data is through market research surveys. Surveys can be conducted by phone, mail, Internet or in person. The key is collecting as much demographic information as possible. The U.S. Census Bureau not only provides information on the U.S.A. but also has an international data base.
  - Demographics change- what effect will ageing, birth rates, immigration, household size, education, occupation, gender, race, employment status, income and health trends have on your business
  - How much of the change in demographics is predictable and how much is not? This is difficult to know since there are so many variables. I believe it best to do your own research using resources, among others, The Wall Street Journal; international, national and state information; demographic websites; mapping tools and articles on the internet.
  - Buying preferences may also vary by geographic region
  - Certain ethnic groups have preferences especially in food and drink

* Economic
  - Proactive economic and financial planning is especially important when dealing with the financial well-being of a company. Having to react to various financial crisis can be fatal. Questions to ask and answer:

- What are the financing requirements for the period?
- In a system, best suited to your team and company, procedures should be in place to forecast revenue, costs, and capital needs
- A system must be in place to measure the budgetary goals.
- Depending on the size of the company, there are various forecasting tools available.
- Lead times and length of the forecast depend on the size and growth rate of a company
* Technological
  o The first thing you must do is ask, what do you use technology for and which functions benefit from technology.
  o Determine that there is a shared vision and the technology meets the needs of the plan
  o The analysis should include cost management, human resources needs, hardware and software, vendor reliance and an assessment of risk
  o After evaluating the strategic plan for the company, a decision may be made that a separate IT strategy should be developed
* Political-legal requirements of the plan should be detailed and driven down into the organization.
  o Prevent overt forms of discrimination
  o Ensure the company is in compliance with all local, state and government laws and regulations
  o Compliance with environmental laws and regulations relevant to the company
  o The company will comply to all labor laws and policies
  o There should be a policy for political activity and political contributions

- There should be a policy concerning trade secrets and confidential information
- There may be other issues that apply to an individual company that should be added.
* Social-cultural
  - Building and managing an effective company culture is a formidable factor in the long- term success of the company
  - Culture is the emotional, organic habitat in which a company's strategy lives or dies [51]
  - The CEO and Senior Management must manage the culture, it doesn't just happen

SWOT ANALYSIS

In a SWOT analysis, each letter stands for one area to review: strengths, weaknesses, opportunities, and threats. Strengths and opportunities are factors within the company, and weaknesses and threats come from sources outside the company. When companies are putting resources and time toward an environmental scan, as previously discussed, they want the results to be as comprehensive as possible. Most scans include a thorough look at competition, economics, technology, legal and financial issues, and social/demographic factors.

REVIEW OTHER COMPANIES' PLANS

The most expedient way to begin crafting a diversity plan after completing the environmental scan and settling on a definition of diversity for your environment is to review the plans of other companies both within and outside your field. It may be that no one plan meets all your needs, thus making it necessary to implement various ideas and approaches from different existing plans. Contacting relevant businesses is important. There are many diversity plans that look impressive on paper but fall flat during implementation. Diversity management is a key to growth in today's fiercely competitive global marketplace. No longer can America's corporations hide behind their lack of cultural intelligence. Organizations that seek global market relevancy must embrace diversity— in how they think, act, and innovate. Diversity can no longer just be just about making the numbers, but rather must be about how an organization treats its people authentically down to the roots of its business model. In today's new workplace, diversity management is a time-sensitive business imperative.[52]

KEY ELEMENTS OF DIVERSITY STRATEGIC PLANNING
The team must develop a strategy to better understand the effects of diversity on productivity and profit in your business and its importance to the business relative to other businesses in your field. Where does diversity rank in importance in your business now? This will require a thourough understanding of your business, how it operates internally, recognizing if diversity is a driver of profitability and if not, how could it be and does your company positively measure up to the competitive leaders of your industry? Where do you want the company to be in three, five and ten years? Do you believe that diversity provides a competitive advantage over your rivals in the marketplace?

Boards play a significant role in both the direction and the image of a company. Currently most boards are primarily made up of white men. Recruiting board directors with a breadth of expertise and varied experiences will make companies more proficient and is just common sense. "A variety of backgrounds can make the company more adaptable to its ever-changing environment"[53] The CEO should plan a high-performance board that is not just diverse in ethnicity or gender just to present a certain image to the public but diverse in capabilities, attitudes and life experiences. This is difficult and may take time but is key in adapting to changing demographics and markets. Tap into the knowledge of the best high- performance boards by researching the elite through resources such as McKinsey & Company, Association of Governing Boards (AGB), Harvard Business Review (HBR) and firms such as Deloitte among others to recognize elements in your board that will make a difference in the board's culture and performance. Work with your board to develop an action plan to ensure everyone is in agreement as you move forward. to go forward.

Chapter 6

THE BENEFITS OF DIVERSE AGES AND GENDERS IN THE WORKPLACE

AGE

When most people think of the word "diversity," attributes such as race, gender, ethnicity, and education immediately come to mind. However, many people overlook the effect and overall benefit of diverse generations in the workplace. When we understand that a diverse, multigenerational workforce can drive revenues, we understand that each generation of workers brings something unique to the business. How can a company use multiple generations most successfully? Is there a more effective way to solicit and develop contributions from each group? Workplaces that combine experienced personnel as well as younger workers can combine years of knowledge with youthful enthusiasm. Businesses that employ workers in ranges of age have the opportunity of having a vigorous, multi-generational staff – presenting a diverse range of skills that is positive for the company.

The American workplace is in a growth spurt, it is rapidly changing, and the old rules may not apply. Your manager might now be younger than you are, and your coworkers may now be an intergenerational mix of baby boomers, gen Xers, and tech-savvy millennials. Think of a family of four or five generations living under one roof and depending on the team for survival. The leaders must develop a team that builds unity across the generational divide. To do this, management must first understand what motivates each segment of the population, what differs, and most importantly, what they share in society. Managers must understand what shaped each generation to avoid the conflict that naturally occurs between them. What is perhaps most striking about is not just the conflict among the generations but the similarity in the negative attributes each generation accuses another generation of having. The key to success in this new environment is developing a plan, using company intergenerational resources, developing relationships, mentoring, and retaining through coaching the knowledge and experience that preserves the legacy of the organization.Unlike a typical human resource plan, our approach to diversity develops and presents a solid business case for more compelling and factual evidence of payback on investment in diversity initiatives. We now see a strong generational imbalance in the workforce, which will certainly continue in the near future. This is very difficult to manage, as language, comportment, and even hygiene may differ. In many cases, there may be years between a younger manager and an older subordinate. If there is a problem, the only way to solve it is to demonstrate both will have a positive result by working together. You can try as you will, but if there isn't something in it for both, the pair will not succeed. These are the hard realities of the modern workplace, where certain skills and experience are no longer needed and managers must redirect associates to learn and accomplish new competences. For this to work the training must be pragmatic particularly if the candidate is a boomer whose experience did not include what is now essential.

Millennials (age 19–34): This generation is perceived as self-absorbed and social media crazed, but they offer great contributions to the workplace. Growing up in an age of advanced technology, they are the ultimate tech junkies, navigating multiple screens, chat functionality, and online forums with ease. Not only are they technologically savvy, but they are excellent multitaskers who are often easily empathetic and understanding of consumers' service expectations.[54] Because they are assertive—some say arrogant—they are effective in working with other assertive people, including vendors. The secret sauce begins here in being able to meld these associates with the other contributors aboard.

Generation X (age 35–55): Despite the buzz around millennial workers, if you're not considering generation X, you are ignoring 60 percent of today's workforce. These workers are loyal, experienced, well-educated and can think creatively. Since most gen-Xers grew up at the beginning of the computer age, they have become accustomed to the technological landscape and can fluidly integrate with their millennial colleagues. Yet at the same time, they can easily relate to baby boomers, who are sometimes inexperienced with advancing technology. Thus, this generation is very versatile, working well with a wide range of clients and customers and helping to strengthen all teams. In addition, per an Ernst and Young survey, members of gen X were cited as the best "revenue generators" among all generations.[55]

Baby boomers (age 56–69): As the oldest members of the workforce, baby boomers are tough, well-oiled machines and often bring a wealth of experience. They recognize what works and can be great mentors when motivated by a collaborative company culture. By bringing generations together, employees step out of their comfort zones and begin to work in partnerships with colleagues from all stages of life. Younger hires, who are less experienced and perhaps less confident, are often open to mentoring advice from workers with more experience under their belts. On the other hand, younger generations can teach older workers how to keep up with ever-advancing technology and evolving social norms. The main diversity challenge, regardless of effort, remains cross generational transfer of knowledge and culture. Many companies focus on mentoring between older and younger employees. As baby boomers stay in the workforce longer and the cultural difference between the generations increases, age diversity is both a challenge and a key to making sure a company's culture stays intact.[56] "Younger workers approach jobs from a completely different perspective, and they have the capacity to gather information and synthesize it quickly which can be potentially dangerous. Company ethics and company values need to be communicated and understood and that takes time. Younger employees run the risk of missing out on important structural aspects and values and procedures which companies have engaged in around their image and brand." [57] In many companies, rolling out the red carpet for generation Y (millennials) is creating intergenerational grudges. Marian Salzman, CEO of Havas PR North America and chair of the Havas PR Global Collective and named one of the world's top five trend spotters, said at an economic conference at Davos, "Baby-boomers really resent these kids." And generation X (born in the mid-1960s to early 1980s) is fed up of being "stuck in the middle between older workers who refuse to retire and younger ones who are treated far better than they ever were."[58] Generation gaps are as old as history. Nevertheless, businesses seem to be more worried than before about managing three age groups with such differing attitudes. A recent survey by Ernst & Young, which asked American professionals from each age group their opinions of each generation, found significant differences, not all of them predictable. Baby boomers, born between 1946 and the mid-1960s, are not slacking off as they age; they are hardworking and productive. The middle ranks of generation Xers, who might be expected to be battling their way up the corporate ladder, are viewed as the best team players. Some opinions on the youth of generation Y are less surprising: they are good at tech stuff but truculent and a bit work shy. [59] Despite the millennials' mixed reviews, many of their number have enjoyed swift promotion into managerial positions. Being "digital natives" has helped them overtake older candidates in jobs where understanding of things such as social media gives them a leg up. Employers may also be promoting them because of three characteristics that often show up in surveys of millennials' attitudes: their demand to be treated meritocratically, their appetite for responsibility, and their unwillingness to hang around if they do not get what they want.

It is very difficult for older male workers to report to a younger boss, either a man or a woman. For women, having a younger male boss is not that unusual while having a female boss is. But both have proven to cause difficulties, as the older generation believes they have paid their dues and time has passed them by. They do not understand the lack of company loyalty, and they do not always recognize the skills younger workers might possess. Younger workers are often more media savvy, are better at multitasking, and enjoy getting feedback from others, something older colleagues might see as criticism if compared to them. For most businesses, it is now imperative to have an internet presence—at a minimum, to have a website and be adept at social media. For most millennials, these skills are natural and expected, but for most baby boomers, these skills must be learned, and impatience from both groups can flare up, causing problems. It is almost like taking a skilled mechanic who has been successful working on Mercedes Benz automobiles and transferring him to work on Teslas. This individual has great skills and has had a great career, but can he or she keep up, and how quickly can he or she learn and assimilate?

The most obvious question, is it worth it? The situation is rife with stress and anxiety. Many millennials believe they are unfairly criticized for having a sense of entitlement, having poor communication skills, and being job hoppers. If they find a company that offers challenging work and a sense of purpose and development, they will stay, says the chief human resources officer at McDonald's Corporation. Both baby boomers and millennials would be well served, as would their companies, if both developed skills at mentoring. [60]

The skills needed to be successful in business are constantly changing, and those changes require teams to be creative, connect with customers, and design their operations for speed and flexibility.[61] Creativity can be taught at any age to any gender at any time. What is needed is team diversity, as diversity is the crucial element for group creativity. Teams whose missions are to create new products or technologies need opposition to produce innovations, and pressure comes from diverse points of view. This is the opposite of groupthink, which is a creativity-killing experience where too much agreement and too many similar viewpoints can paralyze a team. When everyone on the team has been recruited because of similar views, the project tends to fail. Then there is the realization that shared backgrounds and similar experiences doomed the creativity needed for true innovation. When marketers at GE talked about marketing's role being about uncovering customers' value and innovating to deliver it, they found doing so was aided enormously by integrating diverse ideas on a single innovation team. "The problems customers face are often too complicated for any one approach—integrating diverse perspectives from within and even from outside the company may be key to solving them with new breakthroughs." [62]

GENDER DIVERSITY

Men and women often have different perspectives, ideas, and business perceptions, possibly facilitating enhanced decision making and leading to better top and bottom line performance. A gender-diverse team better identifies with an increasingly diverse consumer market.

"This happens because a gender-diverse workforce eases the process of accessing resources, such as multiple sources of information or credit, and industry knowledge".[63] Having a gender diverse company allows companies to hire and retain talented women. To compete in the world marketplace a company must remember that over 50% of the population are women and they must be served to be competitive. Programs must drive home the benefits of gender diversity by ensuring that managers understand the company benefits with better financial results as well as creating a more positive culture that enables men and women to develop supportive associations and influences them to operate at an elevated level. When assessing a company, the presence of an equally balanced and equally paid workforce should begin with gender, since most research shows gender-diverse teams perform better than single-gender teams and will offer the biggest bang for the buck. A more diverse organization provides a more diverse set of skills, especially when one considers the phrase "taking things to heart." which may be a phrase that encapsulates a primary difference between men and women at work. Relational by nature, women take their work relationships personally, and invest in work emotionally. Most women join companies with the desire to be part of a team, to connect with the other players, and to deliver outstanding results. While men are friendly towards their colleagues, women often relate to co-workers, clients, and vendors as friends. [64] " Most companies as well as the government, do not admit that men and women are not equal and not just because in theory men have difficulty seeing women as equals but is an accurate reflection with historical standing. For men and women to be perfectly equal they would have to be the same and it is unquestionable that a man and a woman are not the same, not only physically but in how they see and relate to society. This is a positive, not a negative, as the sexes may be different but are complimentary in many ways when linked. Everything cannot be equal but in the workplace the opportunities and treatment and pay of women should be equal. Society has biases so ingrained that our actions still haven't caught up with our enlightened views. Americans claim to hold equitable views—they know these are the right views to have, much like most people will certainly say they are not racist. But converting such views into practice is another matter entirely.[65]

As politically incorrect as it seems, one could conclude that a business needs to be diverse in nontraditional ways to be creative, and to have employees that are religious and nonreligious, progressive and conservative, and of various age groups, genders and work experiences. This is certainly not the norm when writing job descriptions.

Chapter 7

THE ABCS OF LGBTQ

LGBT is an acronym that originated in the 1990s and replaced what was formerly known as "the gay community." The acronym was created to be more inclusive of diverse groups. LGBTQ, often used since 2015, stands for lesbian, gay, bisexual, transgender, and queer (and/or questioning) individuals/identities.

Today's workforce has become much more diverse in terms of qualities such as race, ethnicity, gender, national origin, religion, gender identity, and sexual orientation. The bottom-line case suggests that such diversity in the workplace will lead to lower costs and/or higher revenues, improving profits. Business has now considered the economic benefits of adding lesbian, gay, bisexual, and transgender (LGBT) policies, including sexual-orientation and gender-identity nondiscrimination policies as well as domestic partner benefits. However, in today's workforce, employees still face persistent discrimination and unfair treatment due to their gender, age, race, and sexual orientation. Glassdoor.com, an online jobs and career community where people share workplace insights, recently ranked the twenty-five best companies for LGBTQ employees. To compile its list, Glassdoor looked at the 250-plus companies on the Human Rights Campaign Best Places to Work 2013 list and compared the companies' overall ratings on Glassdoor.com, which are based on employee-generated reviews from February 2013 through February 2014. "This list underscores the companies where diversity is appreciated, supported, and embraced," says Scott Dobroski, Glassdoor's community expert. "At several of these firms, we're seeing some efforts that specifically support their LGBT employees, from employee groups to community outreach."[66]

More companies are seeking out diversity in their workforce today as they're realizing that a diverse workforce often leads to new ideas and new initiatives, which can only support business objectives. Policies that welcome and encourage LGBTQ associates with voluntarily enacted sexual-orientation and gender-identity nondiscrimination policies, domestic partner benefits, transition-related health care benefits, and other related policies are said to be sound business decisions, in addition to being the fair or right thing to do. Having these benefits and policies and a welcoming environment motivate associates and, according to the Williams Institute's Sears and Mallory, have a positive impact on the corporate bottom line as well as the following:[67]

* Improved recruitment and retention of talented employees
* New ideas and innovations generated by drawing on a workforce with a wide range of characteristics and experiences
* Attracting and better serving a diverse customer base
* Increasing employee productivity
* Securing business with public sector clients that require employment nondiscrimination or domestic partner benefits policies
* Boosting morale and employee relations by responding favorably to requests from employees or unions

Masculine Women, Feminine Men,
Which is the rooster which is the hen?
It's hard to tell 'em apart today.
And SAY...
Sister is busy learning to shave,
Brother just loves his permanent wave,
It's hard to tell 'em apart today.
HEY! HEY!
Girls were girls and boys were boys when I was a tot,
Now we don't know who is who or even what's what.
Knickers and trousers, baggy and wide,
Nobody knows who's walking inside.
Those Masculine Women, Feminine Men [67]

Economic growth in the creative economy is driven by three *T*s: technology, talent, and tolerance. But technology and talent have been mainly seen as stocks that accumulate in regions or nations. Both technology and talent are flows. The ability to capture these flows requires understanding the third *T*, tolerance, or the openness of a place to new ideas and new people. Places increase their ability to capture these flows by being open to the widest range of people across categories of ethnicity, race, national origin, age, social class, and sexual orientation."[69] Diversity provides a richer cultural experience for citizens and visitors, bringing with it openness to new ideas and wider markets and customers. Diverse and tolerant companies are more likely to attract skilled workers who possess the "creative capital" required to power knowledge economies. The most successful companies in the United States and the world have very pro-women, pro-LGBTQ, pro-minority environments, mentorship, flexible work schedules, and great benefits. Most successful companies in the world have diversity and inclusion programs whose goal is to promote a diverse workforce, but only those companies with a committed CEO succeed. Business leaders send a powerful message when they demonstrate a commitment to diversity and inclusion that goes beyond rhetoric. There's a performance-based argument to say that diversity of thought, diversity of perspective, diversity of opinion is crucial. Why? Because the world changes. If you don't have any changes in your marketplace or your competitors, if you don't have any changes in your materials or your workforce, then maybe it doesn't matter. But I don't know of a business like that. One of the ways organizations adapt is by noticing what's going on in the environment and trying new things. How do you come up with innovative ideas, unless you have a spectrum of ideas to examine? With the companies such as Google, Apple, Bain, Nike, Chevron, Ford, McKinsey, eBay, and Hyatt, as well as others, leading the way, one would think business and government would understand the benefits and morality of setting higher standards, which equals higher profits. We believe companies with a diversified workforce in both gender and race outperform those with less diversity among staff. Diverse companies usually are better positioned to get top talent while also better understanding the diversity in their customer populations. Employee satisfaction is also high, leading to a happier workplace devoid of legal issues such as sexual harassment, which remains a problem in corporate America, making gender diversity a tough road. Diversity continues to be needed in the management ranks. It is still predominately male; only 14.2 percent of the top five leadership positions at the companies in the S&P 500 are held by women, according to a CNNMoney analysis. It's even worse if you just consider the very top. Out of 500 companies, there are only twenty-four female CEOs.[70]

DIVERSITY FOR FUN AND PROFIT

According to McKinsey & Company, in a January 2015 article, "Why Diversity Matters, " by Vivian Hunt, Dennis Layton, and Sara Prince, new research makes it increasingly clear that companies with more diverse workforces perform better financially. "We know intuitively that diversity matters. It's also increasingly clear that it makes sense in purely business terms. Our latest research finds that companies in the top quartile for gender or racial and ethnic diversity are more likely to have financial returns above their national industry medians. Companies in the bottom quartile in these dimensions are statistically less likely to achieve above-average returns. And diversity is probably a competitive differentiator that shifts market share toward more diverse companies over time.[71] It is a leadership issue in both business and government. Most businesses are managed implementing short-term goals, quarter to quarter; there is pressure to produce results quickly regardless of the viability of plans and budgets. We see the same thing in our government. The need to be reelected and serve the financial masters trumps most planning, and attracting the best and the brightest to public service just doesn't happen. Why would the best and the brightest want to work in such a confining atmosphere? As of the time of this writing, there is barely a place in the Republican Party for the LGBTQ community and what appears to be little room for minorities, regardless of what leaders say. There is a saying that the proof is in the pudding, and the Republicans are pretty much tapioca. The Democrats may have more diversity when it comes to color and language, but they face the same challenges of money and reelection. The system simply doesn't work, and these same government bureaucrats are setting the rules and regulations for our businesses without any understanding of the true requirements of the private sector. Most companies attempt diversity only to meet legal requirements that have nothing to do with productivity or promoting individuals and building careers and often become a negative rather than a positive. It is hard work to initiate a good and meaningful program, and most CEOs do not believe it is in their best interest. The relationship in this country between business and government is codependent, but the government has really done very little beyond legal and bureaucratic mumbo jumbo to promote diversity. The bond between business and government has weakened and become increasingly hostile since the banking crisis of 2007–8.[72] However the relationship is expected to become more positive during the Trump administration as the President has filled his Cabinet with people from the business world. Congress and the bureaucrats who really run the government know very little about how business works, as most legislators are either professional politicians or lawyers, both professions that can be defined by their lack of flexibility and most government workers have never worked in the private sector. These limitations are seen in the interactions between business and government, which can become labored. The two entities, the legislature and the bureaucrats, are immersed in tax policy, regulations, and in controlling competition by countless regulations, and rarely do they manage their areas productively; if anything, they affect productivity negatively. So much corporate time and effort are required to manage these rules and regulations that only large companies with big staffs and budgets can ensure a successful and productive inclusion program. These same large companies continually attract the best and the brightest, leaving their smaller brethren suffering from a lack of talent. Unless a company is willing to invest in the future and its people, it is most likely doomed to extinction in what is becoming a global marketplace. Employers such as Microsoft claim that nontangible assets, such as intellectual capital, talent, leadership, and reputation, represent 90 percent of their market value. Even in a changing economic climate, qualified LGBTQ employees can take their talent to the most inclusive work environments. In a recent survey of 1,127 LGBTQ people, workplace equality—that is, being able to work in an environment where one can be fully open about one's sexuality or gender identity without fear of discrimination—was rated the single most important issue facing them. So, unless a company has an inclusive and welcoming environment, it is going to miss out on top LGBTQ talent, which will have a negative effect on the business and a positive one on the competitor who understands how to recruit the best talent.[73]

> *Somewhere over the rainbow way up high*
> *There's a land that I heard of once in a lullaby*
> *Somewhere over the rainbow skies are blue*
> *And the dreams that you dare to dream really do come true*
> *Someday I'll wish upon a star*
> *And wake up where the clouds are far*
> *Behind me*
> *Where troubles melt like lemon drops*
> *Away above the chimney tops*
> *That's where you'll find me*
> *Somewhere over the rainbow bluebirds fly*
> *Birds fly over the rainbow. Why then, oh, why can't I?*
> *If happy little bluebirds fly*
> *Beyond the rainbow why, oh, why can't I?* [74]

With skills at a premium, irrespective of the economic climate, holding on to expensively trained, nurtured, and motivated staff is a key priority. Every staff member who leaves an organization because of a negative workplace culture, discrimination, or stress has a potentially negative impact on its reputation as an employer—internally as well as externally. Turnover is harmful to an organization and can take numerous forms, including the exit of high performers and employees with hard-to-replace skills and the departure of women or minority group members, which erodes the diversity of your company's workforce. Australian research (Stonewall 2008) demonstrates that almost two in five LGBTQ staff facing discrimination will change careers if the discrimination continues. Being positive toward LGBTQ recruits is a litmus test for inclusive and effective recruitment. It's not just about attracting the best LGBTQ people; it's about attracting the best people.[75] Despite the progress made toward LGBTQ workplace equality, millions of Americans today go to work fearing losing their jobs because of who they are or whom they love. No current federal law protects LGBTQ workers from employment discrimination. According to surveys, more than 40 percent of lesbian, gay, and bisexual people and almost 90 percent of transgender people have experienced employment discrimination, harassment, or mistreatment. This is not only bad for LGBTQ workers; it is also bad for business.

Presented by *Out Now*, a new study, "LGBT 2020—LGBT Diversity Show Me the Business Case," states that the US economy could save $9 billion annually if organizations were more effective at implementing diversity and inclusion policies for LGBT staff." According to the Business Case for Diversity, today's workforce is increasingly diverse in terms of personal characteristics such as race, ethnicity, gender, national origin, religion, gender identity, and sexual orientation. In turn, it's found that a well-managed diverse workforce will both reduce costs and generate greater profit. Clearly, presenting business owners with an incentive to act and incorporate LGBT-supportive workplace policies makes sense. [76]

BENEFITS FOR INDIVIDUALS

LGBTQ-supportive policies have an immediate effect on individual people, resulting in less discrimination and increased openness about being LGBTQ. According to a survey conducted by the Williams Institute, "The Business Impact of LGBT-Supportive Workplace Policies, LGBT employees who spend considerable time and effort hiding their identities in the workplace experience higher levels of stress and anxiety, resulting in health problems and work-related complaints. Therefore, a LGBT-friendly workplace will lead to improved health, increased job satisfaction, better relationships with coworkers and supervisors, and greater work commitment among LGBT workers."[77]

BENEFITS FOR THE BUSINESS

Benefits to companies may include lower legal costs related to discrimination lawsuits as well as lower health insurance costs through improved health of employees. In today's business world, it is no secret that publicized discrimination causes current customers to leave brands. With the adoption of inclusive policies, the negative public image that discrimination brings would be avoided and attract customers who are eager to do business with socially responsible companies. The company is likely to gain a larger market share among LGBTQ consumers. This is very important, since the number of same-sex households is rising (80 percent increase from 2000 to 2010), as well as the buying power of LGBTQ consumers (an estimated 20 percent increase from 2006 to 2012).[78]

Market	Population	Buying power	per capita
Gay American	16.5 million	$450 billion	$27.3K
African American	30.0 million	$535 billion	$17.8K
Hispanic American	31.0 million	$383 billion	$12.4K
Asian American	11.0 million	$229 billion	$12.0K

Source: Planet Out Partners, 2003 [79]

Furthermore, LGBTQ customers tend to be very brand loyal to companies who reach out to them. In a national survey conducted by Harris Interactive in 2011, nearly nine out of ten LGBTAQ adults (87 percent) said they are likely to consider a brand providing equal workplace benefits. Twenty-three percent of LGBTQ adults have switched products or services because a different company was supportive of the LGBTQ community, even if the second brand was costlier or less convenient. LGBTQ staff who are able to be openly out in front of their colleagues are more likely to remain in their current positions than those who are not. Thus, more effective implementation of diversity and inclusion policies, among other things, saves a significant amount spent on new talent recruitment and training. Furthermore, a more diverse and open workplace increases creativity, which leads to innovation and new ideas. Finally, there is a greater demand for the company's stock because of the expected benefits of diversity policies.

Discrimination based on gender identity is prohibited. Also, many federal contractors have enacted policies on LGBTQ workplace equality. Of the largest fifty federal contractors, 86 percent prohibit sexual-orientation discrimination, and 61 percent prohibit discrimination based on gender identity. In 2007, BP chief Lord Browne resigned from his position after he was outed for being gay and tried to stop the story from appearing in the newspaper. "For the past forty-one years of my career at BP I have kept my private life separate from my business life," Lord Browne said. "I have always regarded my sexuality as a personal matter, to be kept private," he said while stepping down from his function. It was unacceptable back then to be gay in business, and most definitely the oil business.[80] Today, the CEO of Apple, the most closely watched company in the world, has voluntarily stepped out and said, "I'm gay. Being gay has given me a deeper understanding of what it means to be in the minority and provided a window into the challenges that people in other minority groups deal with every day. It's made me more empathetic, which has led to a richer life."[81]

CORPORATE EQUALITY INDEX, THE ROAD MAP FOR ADOPTION OF INCLUSIVE POLICIES [82]

Every year the Human Rights Campaign (HRC) publishes the Corporate Equality Index (CEI), which serves as a road map for major US businesses' adoption of inclusive policies, practices, and benefits for LGBTQ employees. To receive a perfect score of 100, a company must, among other requirements, (1) have an equal employment opportunity policy, including sexual orientation and gender identity or expression, in place; (2) provide equivalent spousal and partner benefits, accompanied by transgender-inclusive health insurance coverage; and (3) provide competency training and resource measures together with either an employee group or a diversity council. In this year's thirteenth edition, a record number of 366 businesses achieved a top rating of 100 percent. In its initial year, a decade ago, only 13 businesses achieved the highest rating. The outreach of the survey has also increased over the years, with 781 companies rated today, including an impressive number of 46 new brands opting into the survey this year.

Recently, many have recognized both the advantages and the shortcomings of such a list. Some question the accuracy of the list of qualifications necessary for gaining the 100 percentage actions and its wrongdoings. A recent lawsuit filed by a transgender woman, Leyth Jamal, against Saks Fifth Avenue shows the persisting gap between what is written on paper and the lived points, while others point out the fact that the index does not consider the larger picture of a corporation's reality. Ms. Jamal was terminated after speaking up against a supervisor's request to not dress and present as a woman at work. The story made the headlines after the response Ms. Jamal received at court. Saks filed a federal motion to dismiss the case because the transgender community was not being protected under Title VII of the Civil Rights Act of 1964. The high-end department store has both protections on the grounds of sexual orientation and gender identity in place. It also scored 100 points on the CEI for several years. While Saks is publicly undermining its own policies, the situation is negating the policies that Saks reported to HRC for the index.[83] With the wave of criticism and the circumstances following Ms. Jamal's suit, HRC is changing the requirements so the CEI addresses diversity and inclusion policies more accurately. Also, concerned with Saks's attitude, HRC suspended the score of 100 for Saks for an unspecified period. We are experiencing a shifting landscape today, where American attitudes and business practices are changing toward a more acceptable and tolerant environment. A rising number of business owners realize that equality is good for business. They acknowledge that their employees need to focus on making the most of their talents and skills, rather than worrying about losing their jobs to discrimination. Still, the gap between policies promoting equality and the reality for LGBT workers is pervasive and striking. In its most recent report, "Accelerating Acceptance," GLAAD (formerly the Gay & Lesbian Alliance Against Defamation) revealed that approximately one out of three non-LGBTQ Americans still feels substantial levels of discomfort with LGBTQ coworkers. To build a workplace where LGBTQ employees are not just tolerated but accepted and welcomed takes more than employing the best nondiscrimination policy and having the largest pride-parade marching group, even though those are steps in the right direction. Earning a perfect score and being labeled the "best place to work" for LGBT people is not going to make the problems LGBTQ people face go away. The change will come through the effective implementation of nondiscrimination policies but also through the deeper understanding and empathy from Americans themselves.[84]

> *Workin' 9 to 5, what a way to make a livin'*
> *Barely gettin' by, it's all takin' and no givin'*
> *They just use your mind and they never give you credit*
> *It's enough to drive you crazy if you let it*
> *Workin' 9 to 5, for service and devotion*
> *You would think that I would deserve a fat promotion*
> *Want to move ahead but the boss won't seem to let me* [85]

Let's look at two distinct industries and their results: the fashion and tech businesses. In both the product must be exceptional and the latest. Many of the employees are frequently customers and therefore often design and market for themselves. How better to understand your customer? This same tenet can apply to any product, assuming the employee mix backs it up. The CEO must be the visionary. Tech leaders are using their voices and influence to speak out on social and political issues.[86] Consider this: all of

Apple's products are based on founder Steve Jobs' belief that the company represented the customer. Apple engineers and designers continue to require that products must be items that customers cannot live without. The products must be understandable and easy to use. At Apple, regardless of the technical proficiency of the customer, the product's ease of use is more important than the product itself. In a fashion apparel business, such as I have worked in for the last 35 years, product development is the number-one priority. The brand's identity must be tested and developed and supported with a marketing and communications plan. The challenges of production must be understood, and a focused sales and distribution strategy developed. As in tech, a variety of talent and experience is needed; a diverse workforce is mandatory.

Apple keeps things simple, and everyone focuses on understanding the one iPhone, iPad, or iPod the company makes and markets. Apple goes against the grain in depth and breadth in understanding consumers, who seem to appreciate this, considering the huge number of iDevices that are sold each year. But a fashion business can miss the market, as J. Crew, considered a successful retailer, has done. To be successful, J. Crew must completely understand the customer and be sure the workforce matches the brand. The question here is, is diversity the problem, or is it too wide a selection or a workforce who's not in love with the product? The future seems to lie in a blend of fashion and technology, creating the need for very diverse staff. FTI Consulting, Inc released its U.S. Online Retail Forecast: Omni-Channel Retailing Challenged by Its Success, which projects U.S. online retail sales will approach $440 billion in 2017, compared to an expected $395 billion in 2016 and approach $1 trillion by 2026.[87] Companies must offer great customer service whether online, in the store, in the catalog, or on social media. Millions are taking service issues to social media making both good and bad comments immediately public. Companies must react to these comments and the ability to relate to a diverse customer base is imperative to the success or failure of a business. Failure to respond to customers can lead to lost customers. An estimated $41 billion is lost by U.S. companies each year due to poor customer service [88] Unlike any other company, Apple takes care of Customer problems immediately. Apple uses this information and makes products better. The company's diverse group of "geniuses" works together, pulling skills to fix every problem. They are dependent on one another for their success; therefore, skills are the priority, not religion, sex, or gender. In my opinion, this is the only criterion that works for building and maintaining a truly productive workforce. Apple stays ahead by working on products at least two years out. Because of Apple's "geniuses" in every area of the business, it stays ahead of the competition by concentrating on fewer products. According to, in celebration of efforts made toward gay, lesbian, bisexual, and transgender rights equality, Apple has added a special section to the iOS App Store pointing to movies, music, TV shows, apps, and other online media it says reflects LGBTQ pride. [89] Perhaps because the CEO of Apple is gay or just because it is smart business, this puts Apple on the cutting edge of marketing.

At J. Crew, the challenge is that while the company has moved up in price in recent years, the rest of the world has shifted down. The rise of fast-fashion chains like H&M and Zara has improved the quality of low-priced goods, making J. Crew's more expensive clothes less appealing. As one of the strategies to increase sales, in addition to going back to lower price points, J. Crew was one of the first retailers to market to the LGBTQ market in 2011 by depicting its head designer and his boyfriend in its catalog. But did the company understand its customers, both gay and straight, or did it misread the economic and fashion cycles? It reported poor sales, with customers criticizing the brand's styles, quality, sizing, and prices. Although the campaign was aimed at the gay community the company J. Crew didn't understand what its customers wanted and the executives who happened to be gay and designed the ad campaigns forgot the basic tenet of retailing "give the customer what they want." Gay or straight was not an issue, the product was simply wrong and marketing can't fix that regardless of diversity.

Chapter 8

UNDERSTANDING THE DIVERSE CUSTOMER— INCLUSION AS A DRIVER OF BUSINESS

When we think of diversity, we don't necessarily see it as a religious issue. However, religion has had and continues to have an enormous effect on workplace diversity. In the past, religion and spirituality had no place in business, but as companies embrace an expanding global economy and increase their sourcing of global job candidates, religious diversity in the workplace is rising. In addition, a growing number of employees are taking their religion and spirituality to work.[94] For management of companies like Hobby Lobby, Tyson Foods, Mary Kay, Anschutz Entertainment Group (AEG), and Timberland, religion is a focus of the culture of the business, and at times these companies are cited as not being inclusive. Some companies telegraph their beliefs, such as Chick-Fil-A and Forever 21, by printing John 3:16 on the bottom of their bags and cups. Religion and spirituality are important to the board, ownership, and associates. For instance, I learned when speaking with Forever 21 management they tithe a percent of their profits to the church. Religious and spiritual diversity should not just be about human resources policies and practices. An organization's ability to recognize, embrace, and function in an increasingly religious and spiritually diverse world might be critical to its sustainability strategy. Religion and spirituality are very difficult to manage in the workplace, and their inclusion is regulated by law.[95] It is best to understand your customer and to be aware of what manner of inclusion might benefit the organization the most. For instance, if there is a large percentage of African Americans in the customer base, you need an organization that understands what motivates this group. Religion and church play as large a part as do age, demographics, gender, music, and other specifics that require a business to understand the group to focus on their needs. Within the group, there are then subsets that require understanding, such as country of origin, income, region, age, gender, and of course exact religion or denomination. The best way to succeed in in a diverse marketplace is to have representatives on board with the talents and skills required to accomplish the tasks required to reach out to these consumers. This is difficult, but the resulting success is the best motivator for building a diverse organization. When a culture is built on each team's contribution to success, individuals are seen in a much more positive manner. To expect people to shed lifelong prejudices and biases because of a government or company edict is not realistic and will most likely not be successful. "The US model of government, which separates church from the state, serves as a guiding principle for how most US corporations operate, yet most companies culture are more secular (with little or no religious influence) than even the government." According to a *Harvard Business Review* article, "The New Path to the C-Suite," CEOs and C-level management need to look at this culture not as an HR directive but as a strategic marketing plan that ties to financial results[96] Building a culture for the organization with a commitment to diversity is the CEO's job and should be a priority. Employees who believe the culture of the business supports their success will also believe their work and the quality of that work is appreciated. Each year, DiversityInc selects the fifty most diverse companies. The forty-three that were public corporations were 24 percent more profitable than the S&P 500. They made up just 7 percent of the Fortune 500 but generated 22 percent of its total revenue.[97] Most companies have policies that address religious discrimination, but few see a diversely religious organization as a positive or a negative. There are many Christian-based denominations, but that is not a consideration in a diverse organization, and unless your customer base is also Christian oriented, a Christian-centric workforce could be detrimental to the business. Many of these businesses try to influence gender and abortion policies and have a conservative bent to them. With the negative political press regarding immigration, companies must be concerned with harassment and not accommodating not only associates but also customers with these backgrounds and lifestyles. Spirituality for these employees is a way of life; their religion and spirituality define who they are. [98]

ETHNIC CHANGE AS A MARKET DRIVER

"The changing ethnic, cultural, and religious mix within Western societies is having a profound impact on consumer lifestyles, shopping behavior, and company strategies," according to Gwen Moran at Entrepreneur.com. "Minority communities often identify with one another based on a boundary that distinguishes them from the majority of the population or other minorities, for example, common ancestry or elements of culture, language, or religion. The key factors affecting the ethnic and cultural mix of populations include people moving more between countries for purposes of work, leisure, or study; migration and asylum; and generally higher birth rates among ethnic communities. Migration is also contributing strongly to the growth of urbanization and to overall population growth in markets where birth rates are sluggish."[99] Although Asians have now surpassed the number of Hispanics immigrating to the United States, most of the growth comes from second-generation Hispanics owing to higher birth rates and better economic conditions.[100] The intense migration of immigrants from Asian and African countries, again combined with their higher birth rates, has led to an extraordinary level of ethnic, cultural, and religious diversity in these markets and is impacting lifestyles and shopping patterns within Western societies. As this is not about to change, regardless of political posturing, companies must learn to market to these new segments of the population. "In 2013, approximately 41.3 million immigrants lived in the United States, an all-time high for a nation historically built on immigration.[101]

"According to the Migration Policy Institute, the United States remains a popular destination, attracting about 20 percent of the world's international migrants, even as it represents less than 5 percent of the global population. Immigrants accounted for 13 percent of the total 316 million US residents; adding the US-born children (of all ages) of immigrants means that approximately 80 million people, or one-quarter of the overall US population, is either of the first or second generation."[102]

Family, age, economics, politics, and environment are just some of the elements that make up humankind, and by the time the individual reaches the workforce, these elements are ingrained in the individual. To attempt to modify each personality to one behavior pattern is an impossible task, although that is exactly what most diversity training programs try to do and most fail. For a company's culture to be built on the customer, one must not only understand the customer but relate to his or her community and way of life. A key to building company culture is participation in the customer's community and the company must rewards associates with promotions and recognition.

If the customer is African -American, the goal for advancement is to better understand the community and understand the importance of the church as a cultural institution. Traditionally, the black church has been a place for creating individual and political change within the black community. From its emergence in the late eighteenth century to its present-day relevance, the black church has served and will always serve as a haven for African Americans, a place to worship together, and a place where African Americans are open to participate in the community. To appreciate the values of the community you must understand the etiquette in churches differs greatly from what many white churchgoers expect; for instance, talking during the service is allowed, even encouraged. In fact, the presiding minister anticipates talking and interruptions from the crowd. Preachers in African American churches use a call-and-response technique. Without understanding and experiencing a service one cannot understand what motivates this potential customer or how to service them. Blacks place more importance than other ethnicities on the inclusion of their cultural heritage and identity in the advertising messages for products purchased.[103] The church is an integral part of African American communal solidarity that began during slavery and has its roots in West African cultural traditions. Dressing in your "Sunday best" is a reality in the black church. Sporting more formal attire is an outward sign of the social respectability all African American churches expect members to exude. Church attendance practically requires formal dress to distinguish members from the nonchurchgoers of the community.[101]

Understanding the importance of the church and dressing for attendance is believed to be why fashion is so important to the African American community and therefore, in my experience as the CEO of Ashley Stewart, a huge opportunity for fashion retailers once their needs are met and understood. By spending time in church (and regardless of race, you will be welcomed), you will learn by your presence what you cannot just read about. And you will enjoy the experience and meet many new friends. Market research awareness among black America must be done on-site, and everyone must participate. Obviously, not all African Americans are the same, but there are many commonalities in experience that the team must understand. This is the key to our method of diversity training: understanding is more important than acceptance. The same research and collection of data must be performed for all multiracial consumers. The African American consumer is changing, with a growing middle class, but understanding what makes them comfortable and providing an environment they will understand is key.

My advisory firm coaches fashion retailers we work with, especially initially, to include ethnic advertising agencies as partners both in marketing strategy discussions and in building individual and systemic processes. Fashion is intrinsically linked with African American women, illustrated best by an article in the *New York Times* by now-retired senior writer Lena William titled, "Black Church Women and the Sunday Morning Hat." [104]

Here are some guidelines learned over time to help you understand your African American customers:

* African American customers are familiar with the negative the shopping-while-black (SWB) experience where black customers are followed around stores as if they are there to steal. A retailer must offer all customers a welcoming and trusting environment whether online or brick and mortar. Service and friendliness are important for the African-American customer and retailers will be repaid with above average brand loyalty.
* Fast checkout and easy ecommerce navigation is a key for all customers but even more so for the black consumer. My experience shows that while this customer enjoys shopping and has fun, she wants to get done quickly.
* Availability of credit is a major factor in choosing a store or website. Although denied by banks and credit card companies, a study by the Federal Reserve Bank of Boston found that customers living in white neighborhoods are more likely to be approved for credit cards than those living in black neighborhoods. [105] Realizing the need for credit in ecommerce, understanding and resolving this issue can have a huge upside.
* The ability to return merchandise is key to this customer as she is often denied this especially in stores. To compete with Amazon, a business must match their return policy. This customer is often asked to check their bags upon entering the store and is limited in number of items allowed in the dressing room. Chain stores in black neighborhoods have cameras, guards and "forbidding" signing that are not

found in their same suburban stores. The stores seem to be afraid of their customers.
* One must understand the customer to deserve their business and loyalty. We learned at Ashley Stewart that getting the fashion and environment right for this customer and matching her lifestyle, figure and economics was the number-one priority and key to our success. But most of all we appreciated her business and ensured that our store was her store.
* 70 percent of African American shoppers enjoy shopping, compared to 50 percent of the general population. The experience is considered entertainment and a pleasant and enjoyable experience must be provided. This is not always the case in this community and often store operations rules such as cameras, bag checks and dressing room minimums make this customer feel unwelcome. There continues to be a significant increase in brick and mortar stores servicing African Americans and the right product and marketing approach will add additional revenue to their line sites.
* An example of understanding the culture and what is important to your customer is the African American community's continued preference of dressing up for the glory of God, an important aspect of a Sunday service. The aesthetic expression through dress and appearance is important to the community and properly marketed provides additional sales while showing an understanding and responsiveness to the community served. To successfully market to a diverse customer base, you should do the following:
    o Research the customer's community to learn what is important in their lives.

- Marketing, product, ecommerce and all areas of the business that touch the customer must be involved in the research.
  - Understand and use the community's language. when communicating in person, online or other forms of media. Research what social media sites pertain to the group you want to reach.
  - Create al partnerships.in the community such as churches, social organizations and charities. I found that becoming part of the community provided inclusion that was directly related to acceptance.

IMMERSION AS RESEARCH

As earlier discussed, Ashley Stewart Stores, where I was the CEO, was focused primarily on middle-class black women. Depending on their positions in the company, our employees had to participate in roundtable discussions, go on church visits, go to community meetings, work in a community charity, go to clubs frequented by our customers, and participate in the foundation the company had formed to aid the community. To do business as a vendor, we asked them to participate financially or volunteer in one of the charities we worked with. It was total immersion, and associates were paid whenever they participated in events as it was considered company time. To really understand your customer, you must recognize what is important to them, and in the case of the African American customers, as mentioned before, church was number one. Too often outside businesses took money out of the community and were resented. We believed in being part of the community and hiring within. A company, that when I began my tenure was mostly men and 80% white two years later won diversity awards as a company that was 97% people of color and 98% women. We became the customer.

RELIGION AND DIVERSITY; HOW THEY AFFECT A BUSINESS

Religion must be considered when building a more diverse workforce. For much of our society and in certain geographic areas religion is a powerful force. We have discussed the importance of religion in understanding the African American Community, so how does one reconcile religious diversity with business, education, income, political orientation, location, and the belief in science. They all are elements that are ingredients in building a corporate culture.

This is an area where diversity for diversity's sake can have a negative effect on a business. How does one fit the following into a work environment?

* Muslims observe five formal prayers each day. The timings of these prayers are spaced evenly throughout the day so that one is constantly reminded of God and given opportunities to seek his guidance and forgiveness.
* Observant Jews pray three time a day. They do not work from Friday sundown to Saturday sundown, and there are many other holidays and fast days when work is prohibited.
* Christians, depending on religiosity, have many holy days and periods: Lent, Palm Sunday, Maundy Thursday, Good Friday, Easter, Pentecost, Advent, and Christmas. Additionally, depending on one's denomination, there can be many more days and periods to observe; and how does a business adapt to atheists, agnostics and other non-believers?

* Asia was the birthplace of many religions, such as Hinduism, Buddhism, Confucianism, Taoism, Jainism, Sikhism, and Zoroastrianism, as well as many other religions, and Asians are migrating to the United States in record numbers.
* The rituals, if any, of these different institutions should accommodate the business and at the same time adhere to Title VII of the Civil Rights Act of 1964 that requires employers to "reasonably accommodate employees' sincerely held religious beliefs, observances and practices when requested, unless accommodation would impose an undue hardship on business operations." This means accommodation and consideration for employees of various religions, be it allowing employees to decorate their personal spaces, scheduling to accommodate employees' religious practices, supplying foods that meet various religion-based dietary needs, modifying the dress code, providing designated space for religious practices, providing paid leave for holidays, or allowing on-site religion-based affinity groups to meet.[106]

It is doubtful that building a diverse workforce would incorporate all the above-mentioned religions and practices but a company must be prepared to do so with not only their employees but an ever expanding, diverse and global consumer.

Chapter 9

THE AMERICAN WAY, THE CORPORATE WAY, THE POLITICAL WAY

- The American Way

> America
> My country, tis of thee,
> Sweet land of liberty,
> Of thee I sing.[105]

The United States of America is the most diverse nation in the world and has been from its inception. Although Mexico, the Caribbean, Canada, Greenland, and South America were all "discovered" in the fifteenth century, only what was to become the United States expanded by absorbing a multicultural population. With Christopher Columbus leading the way, the Spanish government sponsored many of the explorations to the Americas, and as history reports, a less diverse government would have been hard to find. The Spanish Inquisition begun in the fifteenth century continued to function in North America until the Mexican War of Independence (1810–21). In South America, Simon Bolívar abolished the Inquisition. In Spain, itself the institution survived until 1834. Diversity? I think not. Over the first century and a half after Columbus's voyages, the native population of the Americas plummeted by an estimated 80 percent (from around fifty million in 1492 to eight million in 1650). Oh, what to do? Since slavery was banned between Christians, and the Americas were Christian, the solution was to use "pagans" as workers, or slaves. The Portuguese, who were colonizing Brazil, imported millions of slaves to run their plantations. Black African slaves were introduced by the Spanish to substitute for Native labor in some locations—most notably the West Indies, where the indigenous population was nearing extinction on many islands. In 1493, Pope Alexander VI enacted the Inter caetera bull, granting the new land to the Kingdom of Spain in exchange for the conversion of the native population and enslaving them if they refused conversion. Was this the beginning of diversity, the mixing of races, or just felonious assault?[106] This bit of American history helps put things in perspective. Although we are and always have been the most multicultural nation in the world, we have struggled in equality for our citizens. Unlike all other nations, we do not have a dominant nationality. We are related by patriotism, not nationality. We are Polish Americans, German Americans, Japanese Americans, Irish Americans, and so forth, whose cultures all have a commonality or shared attitudes, customs, beliefs, ethics, and value systems. These cultures value their foods, religion, music, humor, clothing, history, and literature. Beliefs and religion also play a significant role—and it's essential we understand this. The diversity game, as it is now being played, does not always consider this ethos, not realizing people may have prejudices based on historical or family precedent. It is all too complicated for managers to deal with; they are expected to do what presidents and government leaders have never been able to do. And yet billions of dollars are spent to train people to be more sensitive to others' needs when the trainers have no idea what those needs are.

Although we are the most culturally diverse nation in the world, we have always been a segregated nation, yet we repudiate the facts. How can we ever relate to African Americans and other minorities if we continue to live, learn, and worship separately? How do "diversity experts" believe they can reverse or modify a lifetime of familial and cultural programming, whether intentionally insensitive or not? Throughout America's history the white race has viewed itself as greater than and superior to others, as men have always viewed themselves as greater than and superior to women. Intentionally or not, we continue to have segregated schools and segregated neighborhoods, and we have always and continue to have segregation in pay equality. Americans grow up culturally and religiously xenophobic with behaviors nurtured by family, friends, and colleagues who are all very much the same.

Land where my fathers died,
Land of the Pilgrims pride,
From every mountainside
Let freedom ring.

Most races have viewed themselves as culturally greater than and superior to others at times. Prejudice is the belief that race is a primary determinant of human traits and capacities and that those racial differences produce the inherent superiority of a particular race.[107] In the case of institutional racism, certain racial groups may be denied rights or benefits or get preferential treatment. According to the UN conventions, there is no distinction between the terms "racial discrimination" and "ethnic discrimination." [108] In many cultures men have always viewed (and continue to view) themselves as greater than and superior to women. How can one cut through this in any diversity training when a large part of the population is indoctrinated since birth to this belief?

* The New Testament states: "But I want you to understand that Christ is the head of every man, and the man is the head of a woman, and God is the head of Christ" (1 Corinthians 11:3–10).
* The Old Testament says: "If [the city] accepts your terms of peace and surrenders to you, then all the people in it shall serve you at forced labor. If it does not submit to you peacefully, but makes war against you, then you shall besiege it; and when the Lord your God gives it into your hand, you shall put all its males to the sword. You may, however, take as your booty the women, the children, livestock, and everything else God has given you" (Deuteronomy 20:11–14).
* The Quran in Sura 4:34 says: "Men are managers of the affairs of women because Allah has made the one superior to the other."[109]
* In the Hindu practice of sati, widows were expected to throw themselves on the burning funeral pyres of their husbands. Women also could not attain moksha, the highest state of being that meant the liberation of the self from the caste system.
* "Buddhism is widely known throughout the world as a religion of peace and kindness. It is less known as a religion of gender-equality. And, in fact, many Buddhists throughout the world are taught that women, because of their characteristic karmic dispositions, are incapable of awakening or of becoming a Buddha, at least without first being reborn as men."[110]

Many Buddhists disagree, believing Buddha's kindness and compassion would have made him incapable of misogyny. However, history tells a different story.[111] Relegating women to second-class status is embedded in religion continuing to this day, many conservative Christians believe women should not work outside the home, and many Muslims believe women are subservient to the point of almost total subjugation to husbands and male family members. Ultra-Orthodox and Hasidic Jewish women are mandated by the men in their lives to be modest in dress and comportment as well as to be subservient to the men in their families and communities. All Orthodox Jewish women's clothing must cover the body at least from the neckline to the knee. After marriage, Jewish women are required to cover their hair because of an interpretation of a biblical law that considers the hair the beauty of a woman, and therefore it shall not be shown in public after marriage. There is no question that in traditional Judaism, the primary role of a woman is as wife and mother, keeper of the household. However, Judaism has great respect for the importance of that role and the spiritual influence that the woman has over her family.[112]

As we have noted, "Religion is a powerful force shaping society." In a country that prides itself on its religious freedom, one must be so very careful when designing inclusion programs. Religion should not just be incorporated into programs to comply with Title VII but should advance an opportunity for open discussion in both training and team building. However, a business must be cautious not to lean in any one direction and should be universal in its approach to make sure the business is not defined by any one belief. A company that accommodates beliefs and opinions of others will usually have a "collaborative and constructive workplace." A religiously diverse business can be more inclusive and becomes more productive as employees are more comfortable being able to be "themselves" and therefore have a high degree of job satisfaction[113].

My native country, thee,
Land of the noble free,
thy name I love.
I love thy rocks and rills,
Thy woods and templed hills;
My heart with rapture fills
Like that above.

Pat Robertson is the founder and chairman of the Christian Broadcasting Network. His website describes him as having "achieved national and international recognition as a religious broadcaster, philanthropist, educator, religious leader, businessman and author." He is a fundamentalist Christian and a leader of his religious community. However, like most of his coreligionists, he is anti-abortion, anti-gay and anti–gay marriage, anti-feminism, anti-Muslim, anti-Hindu, and anti-evolution. Mr. Robertson continues to be a voice for millions of people in this country and perhaps looks on diversity as the work of the devil.

Here are some viewpoints held by certain conservative Christians such as Mr. Robertson: [114] If one subscribes to these theories one might unconditionally accept the Old or New Testaments or they could just be biased and intolerant.

* God hates homosexual behavior as it is prohibited in Leviticus 20:13
* Gays and lesbians try to recruit youths.
* One can "catch" homosexuality at or after puberty.
* Homosexuality is caused by poor parenting.

* Homosexuality is caused by sexual molestation during childhood.
* Homosexuality is an addiction.

Christian and Jewish theologians cite many verses in the Bible that encourage diversity, but it is a diversity that was defined thousands of years ago, and continues to be taken literally. The question must be asked how any religious institution or related practices can be diverse, and in compliance with the EEOC. Most Americans consider the United States a religious county and religious leaders are considered role models. If this is so, a question could be asked: is there an anti-diversity conflict with some leaders desiring diversity to fail in order for more traditional religions to endure? Some Evangelicals appear to have what seems to some an intrusive attitude toward religion in the workplace, they are twice as likely as co-workers to share their beliefs with colleagues. Six out of ten also believe that discrimination against white Christians is as big a problem as discrimination against African-Americans.[115] This presents a problem in both their proselytizing to coworkers and believing they themselves are being discriminated against. The potential for conflict due to this position is significant and could cause workplace difficulties.

MAKING DIVERSITY PERSONAL

Conventional diversity training programs are not sufficiently comprehensive and often target the wrong audience and perpetuate a lack of understanding of diversity's advantages to the individual and the group. A typical American is not especially interested in understanding other cultures. Should we expect a Catholic accounting manager at Bloomingdale's to realize that his Muslim subordinate prays several times a day and must be in the proper environment and position to do so? And what does the Muslim associate think when his supervisor comes into work one spring day with ashes on his forehead, and in a collegial manner advises him he has dirt on his face? How can there be one program covering all? Diversity must be made personal and answer the question, how do I benefit from understanding more about my colleagues and customers?

The Pew Research Center, in a recent study, found that for most employees, money doesn't necessarily buy job satisfaction. Nearly 45 percent of surveyed Americans say having work they enjoy is their greatest professional priority, while about one-third considers job security, work-life balance, and good benefits equally valuable.[115] The same question when asked of employers elicited this response: dependability, self-motivated employees who provide a positive representation of their brand, employees who rise to the occasion, employees with a positive attitude, and employees who are team players. If all the experts and most employees recognize that success is better achieved through teamwork, why is diversity training such a failure? The real question that might be asked is, why is diversity training even needed if it is such an integral part of a job's description and qualifications? Diversity is being scripted by a political correctness that prohibits candid conversations from the lunchroom to the boardroom. We have allowed the quest for diversity to silence disagreement and inventiveness and, in some cases, promote fear of censure or losing one's job. We have perverted a human right by laws, rules, training, regulations, conventions, policies, guidelines, anxiety, appropriateness, intimidation, and exclusion so that diversity has become a negative concept. Diversity and political correctness must be separated at birth; they have no place together in our society. One must wonder what position political correctness should have? It appears it has superseded sound judgment and common sense. If anything, political correctness promotes discrimination by exclusion and is the antithesis of diversity. We cannot cure bigotry with political correctness.[116] Although it is politically incorrect to discuss Nazi Germany in the context of defining political correctness, one could make a case that the virulent anti-Semitism in Hitler's Germany was, by their standards, politically correct and that political correctness was invented there, as one was not allowed to have a point of view other than that of the Nazi Party. Nazis were extraordinarily politically correct but certainly had no incentive to be diverse or accepting of other cultures, religions, and races. Nazi political correctness was the opposite of today's because it was about hatred, not tolerance—Aryan supremacy, not antiracism. What is more insidious: a joke about a rabbi, a priest, and a pastor going into a bar, or six million dead diverse citizens? An extreme comparison, yes, but reality![117]

The Corporate Way

Nine to Five *Tumble outta bed and I stumble to the kitchen*
Pour myself a cup of ambition [118]

The lack of diversity in American corporations should not be a mystery to most of us. We're not used to being in an environment where not everyone is like us. Encouraging those writing job descriptions to include directions to develop an inclusive business culture is not an integral part of most human resource manuals. Diversity is being scripted by a political correctness in an office, factory, showroom, or store where the staff is multicultural, regardless of the product or customer, the boss may not be comfortable and may believe it's his or her right to have his or her "people" around. One would think a business owner or a board would want to take every advantage to make more money. But the deep-seated biases and preconceptions that most Americans have lived with their entire lives are difficult to overcome. Diversity classes are not going to do the job, but understanding the benefits of multiculturalism to the top and bottom line in marketing and sales should. It would be nice to have faith in our virtuousness and trust that our associates and employees will become more sensitive to others through diversity training, but there is very little chance of that happening. Hiring typical workforce diversity experts to come into a business is not going to change anyone or any attitudes, certainly not for the long term.

I worked for a company where a group of women complained to human resources about members of their department talking about their golf game in the break room and at lunch. It was perceived that this was sexist, as the golfers were all men, some in a supervisory role, and the women were not invited to play, thus putting them at a disadvantage. My observation was that there was a bigger problem than the all-male golf group. It appeared to me the underlying problem was a lack of communication and an absence of trust between management and associates. I thought company time was being wasted and that everyone needed a good sit-down to iron out the problem. Simple yes, by knowing what's bothering our coworkers, we will get it in the open and out of the way and be more productive while allowing HR to work on something more beneficial to the associates. But foolish me—enter the diversity manager, and the possibility of sex discrimination raised its ugly head. What followed was a series of meetings and speakers discussing the appearance of discrimination and the effect it can have on an organization. What was never settled was whether there was a problem of discrimination or harassment in the business. Hours and days were taken away from projects, mistrust between associates appeared, and paranoia took center stage. And did the women making the complaint want the men to stop discussing golf at lunch, did they want to golf with the men or did they want them to stop playing together? No one was playing golf on company time, nor was it interfering with anyone's work. We understood discrimination and harassment and had solid programs, and to my best knowledge, it was not part of the culture, nor was it tolerated in the company. There was no answer to this problem that could satisfy everyone and be beneficial to the business. What did the company do? It instituted a company golf tournament allowing for everyone to play golf together on a weekend. In my opinion, the company was now discriminating against nongolfers, applying a bandage to the situation, akin to sitting around the campfire singing "Kumbaya." In my opinion, this was an issue that had no place in HR or in any company department, and I tell this cautionary tale to ensure that diversity programs have a positive and not negative effect on the workforce.

THE FOCUS OF PRIVATE EQUITY FIRMS AND DIVERSITY

Private equity is financing provided in return for an equity stake in potentially high-growth companies. Yet, instead of going to the stock market and selling shares to raise capital, private equity firms raise funds from institutional investors, such as pension funds, insurance companies, endowments, and high-net-worth individuals. Private equity firms use these funds, along with borrowed money and their own commercial acumen, to help build and invest in companies that have the potential for high growth. In 2015, private equity firms did over twenty thousand deals and raised over $300 billion.[119] I believe one of the obstacles hindering corporate diversity and understanding its positive influence on the bottom line is the rise in businesses' ownership by private equity firms. Not understood by the public and with no exact statistics compiled, the equity funds and firms may well have a hand in managing over twenty percent of the companies the U.S. Private equity firms tend to be mostly conservative and thinking about diversity as a contributor to profits does not play a part in their deals, nor is the benefit of diversity in any business rarely, if ever, a consideration. As a matter of fact, equity people, primarily white men, are mostly observers. Regardless of portrayals in movies, on TV, and in books, private equity firms have very little practical knowledge of any business other than deal making and leveraging capital. Many believe money and a business school degree are the keys to success. Rarely do these individuals acquire management experience and skills working for a company. It's as if a person who never played the game of baseball at any level above Little League and whose only experience was as a fan was made the general manager of the New York Yankees. Only in the private banking industry does practical experience mean so little. And yet the influence these firms have on the American workforce is greater than any union. Private equity firms use very little of their own cash or equity to buy into a company, instead borrowing and loading up the company with debt. The private equity firm is not responsible for the debt; the business is, and that now becomes the all-encompassing mindset of the corporation's management. Since private equity firms want their investments returned on an average of five years, there is no time to build a meaningful culture in the business. Short-term results are all that matters. This mind-set is the same in many public companies, where the next quarter's numbers constitute long-term planning.

> *Jump in the shower and the blood starts pumpin'*
> *Out on the streets, the traffic starts jumpin'*
> *With folks like me on the job from 9 to 5*

Over the years, many American businesses have become short-sighted—not investing the time, let alone funding the programs, that would build and sustain a diverse culture. Most consumer businesses do not even do the requisite research to better understand their customers, as often ownership's expectation does not allow them the time to do so. These managers believe investing in diversity just for the sake of diversity is a poor investment not realizing the marketing potential of reaching customers and increasing sales and profits. A diverse management team and workforce better understands the customer consequently increasing the value of the investment and the return.

MARKET STUDY

Although segregation is illegal, its remnants are alive and well across most of the United States. Because so many of our neighborhoods and cities are isolated and ghettoized, we have segregated schools and segregated housing. And to serve these neighborhoods and communities, thousands of businesses market and sell specialized products developed for these narrow but lucrative markets. To be successful in selling to these specific demographics, a company must understand the customer. But is this really diversity marketing or the exact opposite? African American women present a challenge to non-black-centric businesses. African American women spend three times as much on fashion apparel and hair goods as nonblack women, or projected sales of half a billion dollars on hair care alone.[120]

A few years ago, my advisory firm was hired by a minority-managed private equity firm to assess one of its companies. The business consisted of a chain of women's retail stores catering to plus-sized African American women. The members of the equity group were African American, as were the customers of the company they owned. Yet the company was failing because management didn't identify with the customer. The equity group applied a B-school solution of what they believed was a strong management team, a sustainable competitive advantage, multiple avenues of growth, reasonable capital-expenditure requirements, and favorable industry trends. But in their due diligence, they missed the most important characteristic: *Who is the customer, and what did she want?* Over the years, a $100 million investment had been made, but the business was losing $75 million in the current fiscal year. As we began our evaluation, it became clear that the product was not right for the customer. It seemed there was no understanding of the end use of the merchandise via the professional or social life of this customer. Nor was there any consideration for skin tone or a "thicker" body type. A study by Mount Sinai Hospital in New York explains that African American women and men view the heavier female body types as more attractive compared with white counterparts, who prefer a thinner body type.[121] The apparel in the company's stores did not reflect this belief. Moreover, this consumer had a need for styles for church, holidays, and community events that were being completely ignored. Even worse, the stores were uninviting with cameras and security guards and requiring incoming packages to be checked. Obviously, the company management and even the African American private equity owners did not understand or trust the customer. How could a retailer be so far off course? A few weeks later, we made our first visit to the home office to meet the executive management group. Sitting around the conference room table were seven white men and one white woman. There was only one black buyer in the organization. No one in the room identified with the customer or understood her needs. This company demanded a more diverse organization to survive, let alone prosper. Recruiting a staff that matched the customer was immediately implemented. A training program was necessary and not a typical out-of-the-box program but one that hired people from the community and sent associates into the community churches, clubs, and organizations to learn about the customers. A very specific targeted program was needed to fix this business. One year later, with a racially mixed management team and buying staff and more people in the business that looked like the customer, the company posted an $18 million EBITDA for the year, a $93 million reversal. Management was rewarded with bonuses and raises, realized a personal reward and learned a valuable lesson about marketing. The following year Black Retail Action Group (BRAG) awarded the company its corporate diversity award. It wasn't enough that the equity firm's managers were minorities; they were too distant from the customer and had applied the conventional private equity methodology. Most private equity firms ignore diversity, even when their investments centers on an identifiable culture, probably not because of any biases or prejudices but because it isn't included it in any business model. It is not seen as relevant to the numbers.

Workin' 9 to 5, what a way to make a livin'
Barely gettin' by, it's all takin' and no givin'
They just use your mind and they never give you credit
It's enough to drive you crazy if you let it

The Political Way
This Land Is Your Land [122]

This land is your land. This land is my land
From California to the New York island;
From the redwood forest to the Gulf Stream waters
This land was made for you and me.

Like no other election in recent memory, the primaries and lead-up to the 2016 presidential election invaded the workplace and water cooler conversations with talk about walls, immigration, equal pay, minimum wage, and refugees. These topics touched on discordant aspects in our society and morphed into conversations about protected classes that may have been offensive to some associates. What could start as a genial conversation could turn into a heated debate about the candidates or the campaign. Employers and employees should know what they can do or are prohibited from doing in an election season.[123] In a year such as 2016 with had so much dissatisfaction on all sides, the attention on the election had never been greater.

Have we really come as far as we think we have in the political world? To politicians, diversity is just a catchword. How else to describe the numerous caucuses (an exclusive meeting of the members of a party or faction for organizational and/or strategic purposes) formed in Washington to further their own causes?

Informal congressional groups and organizations of members with shared interests in specific issues or philosophies have been part of the American policy-making process since colonial times. Typically, these groups organize without official recognition by the chamber and are not funded through the appropriation process. The growth in the popularity of caucus groups is mostly a phenomenon of recent times. Although caucuses have existed since 1959, they proliferated rapidly in the late 1970s and into the 1980s, and again in 1995. Today there are 173 congressional caucuses, the largest number to be active at any time. Most of these (107) are House caucuses, a minority (25) is in the Senate, and the rest (41) are bilateral.

Here are just a few of many:

House Caucuses
* Congressional Democratic Caucus
* Congressional Women's Caucus
* Congressional Hispanic Caucus
* Blue Dog Coalition
* Caucus of House Conservatives, Republican Study Committee
* Congressional Asian Pacific American Caucus
* Congressional Bike Caucus
* Congressional Black Caucus
* Congressional Center Aisle Caucus
* Congressional Cuba Democracy Caucus

Congressional caucuses are generally associated with the House. Senators are often involved with them as well. In many cases, members of the Senate as well. In many cases, as well. In many cases, as well. In many cases, members of the Senate serve as members on House caucuses. members on House caucuses.

Some Senate Caucuses:
* Senate Democratic Caucus
* Senate Republican Caucus
* Senate Caucus on Missing, Exploited, and Runaway Children
* Senate Taiwan Caucus
* Senate Women's Caucus
* Senate Caucus on WMD Terrorism
* Senate Caucus on India
* Senate Caucus on International Narcotics Control (the only officially recognized caucus)

What is the purpose of the Black Caucus in the twenty-first century? It describes itself as organization of African American members of the US House of Representatives. Founded in 1970, it addresses legislative concerns of African Americans and other minority citizens, such as employment, welfare reform, minority business development, and expanded educational opportunities. The Congressional Black Caucus Foundation (established 1976) conducts research on issues affecting African Americans, publishes a yearly report on key legislation, and sponsors issue forums, leadership seminars, and scholarships. Is there still a need for a group like this, subsidized by taxpayers? What would the reaction be to a Congressional White Caucus?

The purpose of the Congressional Progressive Caucus advocates "universal access to affordable, high quality healthcare," fair-trade agreements, living wage laws, the right of all workers to organize into labor unions and engage in collective bargaining, the abolition of significant portions of the USA PATRIOT Act, the legalization of same-sex marriage, strict campaign-finance-reform laws, a crackdown on corporate welfare and influence, an increase in income tax rates on the wealthy, tax cuts for the poor, and an increase in welfare spending by the federal government. Whew! And there are eighty members fighting for these causes. When do they have time to govern?

And then there is the conservative social and economic agenda in the House of Representatives. The Republican Study Committee is dedicated to a limited and constitutional role for the federal government, a strong national defense, and the protection of individual and property rights and the preservation of traditional family values.

As I was walking that ribbon of highway,
I saw above me that endless skyway:
I saw below me that golden valley:
This land was made for you and me.

The various caucuses couldn't have more different agendas, and yet they are all members of our Congress determining our future—each with distinctive strategies and each self-serving. Is it all about politics, religion, or nationality? Respect, tolerance, appreciation, and concern are the basis for understanding and acceptance of diversity. Our society equates these attributes as "liberal"—not universal—attributes, and this is a conundrum in that we have politicized diversity. African Americans are Democrats. Hispanics were Republicans but are now becoming Democrats, unless you are Cuban American, and then you might be a Republican.[124] As a group, Asian Americans lean toward the Democratic Party, but many are Independents. About 32 percent identify as Democrats, 14 percent as Republican, 19 percent as independents, and 35 percent as nonpartisan. American Jews—73 percent of them, at least—describe themselves as moderate or liberal; 23 percent label themselves as conservative. There are indications that Jewish support for the Republican Party is on the rise. The growing Orthodox communities in the New York metropolitan area and elsewhere are distinctively Republican.[125] Democrats are considered the more liberal of the two major parties since roughly half of the Democratic voter base considers themselves liberals or progressives. Seventy-two million voters are Democrats. Liberals thereby form the largest united typological demographic within the Democratic base. According to the 2008 exit poll results, white-collar, college-educated professionals were mostly Republican until the 1950s; they now compose perhaps the most vital component of the Democratic Party. Most progressives favor universal health care, with many supporting a single-payer system. Immigration and cultural diversity is deemed positive; liberals favor cultural pluralism, a system in which immigrants retain their native cultures in addition to adopting their new culture. They tend to be divided on free-trade agreements and organizations such as the North American Free Trade Agreement (NAFTA). Most liberals oppose increased military spending and the display of the Ten Commandments in public buildings. The Republican Party includes fiscal conservatives, social conservatives, neo-conservatives, moderates, and libertarians. Fifty-five million voters are Republicans.[126] Most the GOP's national and state candidates are pro-life, oppose elective abortion on religious or moral grounds, and favor faith-based initiatives. There are some exceptions, though, especially in the Northeast and West Coast states. They are generally against affirmative action for women and some minorities, often describing it as a quota system, believing that it is not meritocratic and that it is counter-productive socially by further promoting discrimination. Some in the religious wing of the party support voluntary organized prayer in public schools and the critiquing of evolution theory via "intelligent design" in science classes. The party is predominately white and 47 percent male, making it the less diverse of the two major parties.

> *I've roamed and rambled and I followed my footsteps*
> *To the sparkling sands of her diamond deserts*
> *And all around me a voice was sounding:*
> *This land was made for you and me.*

The Tea Party, an offshoot of the Republican and the Libertarian Parties, advocates reducing the national debt and federal budget deficit by reducing government spending and cutting taxes. Eighteen percent of Americans identify as Tea Party supporters. Most them, 89 percent, are white. Just 1 percent is black. Tea Party activists tend to be even angrier, and more pessimistic about the country, and were more negative about President Obama than other Americans who identify as Republicans.[127] The Tea Party came into prominence with the election of Barack Obama as president and many consider black people to have an unfair advantage in dealing with the federal government.[128] An independent may be variously defined as a voter who votes for candidates and issues rather than on the basis of a political ideology or partisanship; a voter who does not have long-standing loyalty to, or identification with, a political party; a voter who does not usually vote for the same political party from election to election; or a voter who self-describes as an independent. Independents compose 40 percent of the electorate, or approximately eighty million voters.[129] There is not a definitive independent movement, as some classify themselves as liberal, conservative, moderate, and some are members of the Tea Party.

DIVERSITY FOR FUN AND PROFIT

The political environment of the Obama presidency may have been the least diverse in many ways than any in the last century. A refusal of the political and media worlds to acknowledge racism not only existed but had increased was mind boggling considering the evidence. What other president experienced the lack of respect from Congress and other politicians? Historically, most arguments between politicos were about policy, but the rancor between President Obama and the Republicans was personal and mean spirited. There seems to have been a hatred of the president by many Republicans, with notable expressions of disrespect not seen before during a State of the Union address. In President Obama's first term, the Republican leader in the Senate said the most important goal he had was to make the current president a one-term president, and Congress tried unsuccessfully to repeal the Affordable Care Act over fifty times and continues this strategy into the Trump administration. These actions do not bode well for the enhancement of diversity in the United States. The populace sees their government as insincere and focused only in its own interests, not those of the citizenry who elected them. How can government programs succeed when lawmakers are rendering them spineless and ineffective? We as Americans must confess to the prejudices inherent in our history and in our society. By denying these traits, we will never succeed in having equal opportunity and pay for all our citizens. Our government needs a massive retraining program. If government were a business, any business, and repeatedly operated at a deficit and with its inability to get anything done, everyone would be fired, after the company filed for bankruptcy. If the discrimination demonstrated by many members of government occurred in a business, these people would be found guilty, lose their job, and perhaps even go to jail. Yet this is what serves as a model at the highest level for diversity in this country. We need to do better, and *Diversity for Fun and Profit* assures the players learn how to improve their skills and discover how to be interdependent on one another to engender success not only for themselves but for the team. It's all about putting the team together to fit the needs of the project and not attempting to convert the infidels.

CASE STUDY: THE OBAMA CAMPAIGN

One of recent history's greatest marketing campaigns was conceived for the 2008 election of Barack Obama. In the 2008 and 2012 campaigns, The Obama staff mined information describing particular voters (an Obama voter), identified them, and understood exactly how to get those voters to act as they wanted them to. The campaign managers had done the research to define who the voters were and where they were, and by applying certain attributes, they designed a program that produced data that directed volunteers to the right doors on which to knock. And those volunteers could identify with the voters because they mirrored those voters. If a speaker was needed for a meeting in a Boca Raton retirement community, a Jewish volunteer would be chosen. If they were campaigning in Miami, the volunteer was Spanish speaking. And if it was a Catholic Charities organization, the volunteer was Catholic. The diversity in the campaign was in first understanding the diverse "customer," matching that customer with the messenger, and then marketing to that customer with an identifiable message. Where McCain supporters were whiter and older, Obama's were younger and multiethnic; those were the doors that were knocked on, and the research and data told the volunteers where they were. That election was about diversity, and diversity determined the overall trends. Republicans were using an obsolete marketing model, and the demographics did not match it. The population was less white, younger, and becoming a minority nation. If Republicans continue to use the same message as in the last two elections, they are most likely going to eventually go out of business. President Obama, was named *Advertising Age*'s marketer of the year for 2008.[130] He edged out runners-up Apple, Zappos.com, Nike, and Coors to manage the most successful "sales campaign" of the year and set the stage for the next four years. President Obama won the vote of hundreds of marketers, agency heads, and marketing-services vendors who were gathered at the Association of National Advertisers' annual conference. His team won by understanding the voter, because they were the voter. This may be the best example of diversity marketing—with the big prize being the presidency of the United States. The success was a combination of data mining to discover patterns in the USA voter population, and but to accomplish that goal the campaign staff had analyzed regional and national voting patterns from different perspectives and summarize it into useful information to affect the marketing effort. If one looked at the Obama campaign volunteers and staffers, one saw groups of people who identified with the candidate and the voters as well as the future and not the past. The campaign did what any company can do: it developed a single, comprehensive database; it hired and trained the right people, people who matched and identified with its target; it tested before committing and eliminated the numbers game; its people understood how the voter/customer would react; it provided a swift and streamlined presence online and in social media; and when it did advertise, it did so on less traditional programming, such as *Sons of Anarchy*.

To promote the Affordable Care Act to young people, President Obama appeared in an episode of the online talk show *Between Two Ferns* with comedian Zach Galifianakis in a successful attempt to connect with young people. He also communicated through Facebook, MTV, and Black Entertainment Television. The president and his staff knew they had to reach the young voters integral to the success of the law, because they were necessary to offset the higher medical costs of older people. The president's opponents criticized these methods with the *National Review*, writing, "The White House pushing the president in the entertainment world is folly." His goal with his appearances was to sign more young people up for Obamacare, and he succeeded by understanding what this "customer" watches, reads, and listens to. The campaign was a success. If the Obama organization and methodology were established in a consumer business, the success of the marketing and sales efforts would be extraordinary.

This is a prime example of diversity for fun and profit at its best.[131] Let us consider the two major political parties as brands; the Republican brand and the Democratic brand. In my consultancy firm, the first step we take when working with a new client is an assessment of their business. This involves evaluating every aspect of the company: the framework, processes, and image. One step in the assessment is a brand audit, where we examine every facet of the brand to see what is working and what is not. Normally, a 48 percent market share would seem admirable, but since there are only two brands in the category, the 52 percent of the market share by the Democrats could be fatal for the Republicans. Reviewing the followers and members of each party would be another step in our process. Republicans are thought of as predominantly white, male, older, wealthier, oppressive to women, conservative, and out of touch with modern society. Democrats are thought of as younger, inclusive to women, diverse, in touch with society, and less wealthy and more financially middle of the road.[132] This Republican demographic is becoming a smaller portion of the populace while the Democratic Party profile is viewed as more appealing to growing segments of the voter population and is more inclusive. The Republican Party desperately needs to rebrand and be more all-encompassing, but the leadership is old, conservative, white, and male. [133] The Republican win in 2016 may prove to be just a blip in history. As a marketing study we ask can a product that fewer people want to buy each year and the younger generations have little interest in last? Think about the products that have faded into history in just the last century; dial phones, film, VCR's, Pan Am, Woolworths and so many more. What is going to make the Republican Party relevant in the future. They need a complete re-branding if they are to survive. The party leadership must become more diverse before the party can successfully transform into a perennial national winner. The brand needs a new personality such as Ronald Reagan provided. The Republican Party tone is often viewed as extreme and angry. Therefore, a new brand premise would be accompanied by a brand personality that is more reasonable, optimistic, and welcoming, and less extreme and scolding. For long-term success, politicians must be located who will be representative of the new brand and be able to communicate a fresh message. People must be recruited who will exemplify and support the new brand, people that come from all walks of life and represent all ethnicities and all genders. This must be the goal of both parties for our political system to be viable.

According to a NBC News/Esquire poll, over 49.7 percent of the country approves of gay marriage, 63 percent support abortion in the first trimester, and 52 percent support legalizing marijuana. They also support a strong, regulatory support system—67 percent support a minimum wage at $10 or more, 62 percent support paid sick leave, 70 percent support paid maternity leave, and 57 percent support tax-subsidies child care to help women get back to work."[134]

We have learned, regardless of Tea Party and Trump rhetoric, that common ground is found where a diverse and growing majority is bound by a surprising set of shared ideas—ideas that are moderate in tone. The Republican party is destined eventually to go down in defeat unless it stops being the "stupid party," as former Louisiana governor Bobby Jindal implored the GOP. Unless it diversifies and becomes more like its "customers," it will lose on a national level, and it won't be fun, and it won't be "profitable."

Chapter 10

AYE-AYE, SIR...ER, MA'AM THE ELEMENTS FOR BUILDING A DIVERSE WORKFORCE AND CULTURE

In the military and in the Navy, it's important that we are a diverse organization because we have to represent what I call the face of America. As our population changes and the percentages of majority and minority change, and that's always taking place, we have to reflect that same demographic in our Navy and that's why it's important, but at the end of the day, it really makes a huge difference because we're stronger because of the different perspectives and ideas that people bring to bear.

—Chief of Naval Operations Adm. Gary Roughead, February 27, 2009

"Anchors Aweigh," 1906 original version[135]
Stand Navy down the field, sails set to the sky;
We'll never change our course, So Army you steer shy-y-y-y.
Roll up the score, Navy, anchors aweigh!

Sail Navy down the field and sink the Army, sink the Army gray!
Get underway Navy, decks cleared for the fray;
We'll hoist true Navy Blue, So Army down your gray-y-y-y;
Full speed ahead, Navy; Army heave to;
Furl Black and Gray and Gold, and hoist the Navy, hoist the Navy Blue!
Blue of the Mighty Deep; Gold of God's Sun
Let these colors be till all of time be done, done, done,
On seven seas, we learn Navy's stern call:
Faith, Courage, Service true, with Honor, Over Honor, Over All.

"America's Navy starts in our own neighborhoods, with our people, our opportunities for growth and success, and our culture, we recognize that diversity offers an exceptional way for the Navy to strengthen itself, and we support and encourage it in our ranks at every level, including senior leadership."[136] The US Navy has been strongly promoting diversity since 2008, when Vice Adm. Kevin McCoy became commander of the Naval Sea Systems Command (NAVSEA). Admiral McCoy was quoted in a 2013 article saying that "one of my key people goals was for NAVSEA to become the Federal Employer of Choice."[137] Part of that goal was to ensure that they fostered a welcoming environment and that assignments and promotions were transparent and merit based. Workplace diversity needed to simply be part of the way they did business every day. The navy definition of "diversity" is "all the different characteristics and attributes of individual sailors and civilians that enhance the mission readiness of the Navy. Every leader understands the importance of diversity and having a diverse workforce."[138] The navy is on a mission to increase collaboration, strengthen its internal support infrastructure, and expand its multicultural partnerships through its Command Managed Equal Opportunity (CMEO) Program. This program is designed to ensure that merit, ability, performance, and potential lead to promotions. The vice admiral leads a staff and workforce of more than fifty-eight thousand sailors and civilians, and in 2010 he and his staff conducted a top-down review of the organizational demographics and the path to hiring and promoting personnel into key leadership positions in the navy. The results showed that while the command understood and embraced diversity, in practice they were missing the mark with respect to recruiting women and minorities and advancing them to leadership positions. To understand and develop a path to change and reverse the trend, he and his executive director implemented annual diversity accountability reviews patterned after those conducted by the CNO (chief of naval operations). In the first assessment, he asked his field activity commanders for an honest appraisal of the state of diversity in their organizations. They looked at the following:

* Identifying key leadership positions and grade levels
* Identifying the pathway an employee would take to get those positions
* Defining how the organization makes employees aware of these career pathways
* Identifying any systemic barriers or cultural norms that prevented the command from integrating diversity into their organization

These initial assessments allowed NAVSEA/PEO Headquarters and Field Activities to self-identify barriers to improving the diversity of the workforce and to lay out a set of actions. The results of these reviews revealed that despite command rhetoric about practicing diversity, the navy was not moving the needle in hiring and promoting diverse personnel, largely because the eligible pool of candidates lacked diversity. They discovered that senior leadership was not directly involved in the recruiting and hiring processes, managers lacked an understanding of the importance of hiring a diverse workforce, and hiring officials were hiring and promoting people who looked just like themselves. Additionally, they uncovered instances where diverse personnel were migrating off traditional technical leadership paths and self-selecting other career paths (e.g., business and finance) for better promotion opportunities. This was a result of perceived reduced promotion opportunity in their technical career paths. The next step was to determine the factors that led to this situation and implement measures to change the culture within the organization. The assessments showed the following as the factors hindering the navy in increasing minorities and women in key leadership positions:[139]

* Minorities and women were not in gateway positions that would lead them to be considered for key leadership positions.
* Women had migrated out of technical career paths to business operations positions, thereby eliminating them from consideration.
* Women and minorities had limited access to high-visibility assignments to continue to progress in their careers.

There was a general lack of succession planning to identify positions that would lead to senior/executive level positions and an absence of cross-cultural mentoring to discover talent and bring it along the career track.

* In the shipyard, blue-collar positions, they found that females were being selected for the apprenticeship programs at significantly lower rates than males.
* Recruiting and promotion processes (interviews, exams, selection board makeup) had not been rigorously reviewed and influenced by senior leadership to ensure that no demographic was disadvantaged. They were hiring and promoting personnel the way they always had, even though diversity metrics were not reflective of the broader population surrounding their activities and were not improving.[140]

In 2010, the diversity practice of our advisory, ESA Associates, LLC, was asked to offer a comprehensive proposal to the Diversity Directorate of the US Navy to address diversity recruitment, programing, and staff development. We were asked to address three specific areas of need:

* Develop a "message that connects" with the relatively untapped Asian American and Hispanic American markets for the US Navy, with the goal of attracting, recruiting, and retaining high-quality STEM talent and officer candidates.
* Enhance and measurably increase the skill sets and competencies of ERG (employee resource groups) leaders, members, and other groups with the US Navy through diversity education and training.
* Provide unique marketing and consulting opportunities to the US Navy by using culturally relevant awareness and outreach initiatives, messaging, and programs to identify and recruit the best and brightest potential enlisted and officer candidates among Asian American and Hispanic communities.

We found the Navy more advanced than many businesses we worked with in the corporate world in terms of promoting diversity, and it had extensive resources, including hiring one of the top advertising firms in the country but still it lacked an understanding of who these candidates were. To accomplish its strategic diversity mission and focus, the Navy needed to recruit and retain the best-qualified and most diverse candidates in concurrence with the criterions of skill sets and competencies of Navy leadership. These elements in leadership had to be in place to support the navy's commitment to continuously addressing it's goals through an effective range of programs to meet their goals and objectives. Over 48 percent of enlisted personnel were minorities, a number much higher than in the US demographics, but only approximately 20 percent of officers were minorities. Specifically, the Asian American and Hispanic populations were underrepresented in both enlisted and officer forces. What we initially found was a lack of understanding or appreciation by either the navy or its resources in understanding the cultures and subcultures of the targeted communities. The lack of recognition of major distinctions in Asian and Hispanic cultures hindered identifying the beliefs, knowledge, values, and behaviors of each specific culture and subculture. Without this understanding, it was impossible to reach each of the target markets to significantly influence their decision making. Hispanic Americans, or Americans who identify as having origins in Spanish-speaking countries, include people of Puerto Rican, Mexican, Cuban, Dominican, South and Central American, or other Spanish speaking cultures. Asian communities include, Chinese American, Filipino American, Indian American, Vietnamese American, Korean American, Japanese American, and others. Comprehensive research, assessment, and evaluation were required to craft the most effective messaging to best appeal to the navy's needs. Psychological and sociological profiles of each culture and subculture were required. To further complicate the assignment, the definition of diversity was not limited to race, gender, and age, and the case for broadening the definition was built on the ongoing changing of labor force demographics. The statistics (as compiled by the Bureau of Labor Statistics and others) are compelling. Here are some facts:

* By that year of 2010, the Hispanic labor force was larger than the African American labor force (13.3 percent versus 12.7 percent). Asians continued to be the fastest-growing group in the labor force increasing by nearly 45 percent this decade.
* Women currently compose nearly half of the labor force. Most workers entering the workforce in that decade were women, minorities, and foreign nationals.
* The labor shortage that began in the 1990s will continue to grow and had reached ten million workers by 2010.[141]

DEFINING CULTURE

Culture is defined and interpreted in many ways. When attempting to influence and build cultures, it is imperative to know how others send and interpret information. To that end, Edward Hall, a highly-regarded expert on intercultural interaction, identifies two dimensions of cultures— (1) collectivistic or individualistic and (2) high or low context—that significantly affect the persuasive messaging among and within ethnic communities.[142] Individualistic versus collectivistic individualism (or collectivism) is one of the dimensions of national culture identified by several researchers. It is commonly seen as a basic value that distinguishes members of different cultural groups from one another. It relates to the relative emphasis that members of a society place on their self-interest versus that of other groups. In a collectivist culture, people tend to define themselves in terms of their relationships with others and are more inclined to give up their individual needs when there is a conflict between their needs and group needs. In an individualist society, people tend to define themselves as autonomous entities independent of a group. People in this group tend to be more competitive. People in a collectivist culture tend to share their knowledge and place the interests of the collective over their own. [143] North Americans are identified as individualistic, while Asian and Hispanic cultures are identified as collectivistic. The US military, with its emphasis on the success of the group, would be considered a collectivistic subculture within an individualistic culture. Although there have been varying levels of adaptation to the dominant US culture, we theorized that the commonality of collectivism as a core value in both Asian and Hispanic cultures (with the common themes being the values of the US military) would provide a theoretical foundation for the navy messaging and recruitment strategies. Without the understanding of the various cultures, along with a paucity of representatives of the cultures in officer ranks, the work would have to be performed mostly by civilians and the small group of representative personnel. As discussed throughout this book, I believe one must have a diverse organization to effectively target a diverse customer. There is, no such thing as an Asian American. There are Korean Americans, Indian Americans, Japanese Americans, and so on. The history and customs of these cultures must be understood to understand how to approach each. Culturally, there has been little unity or common history for many of the cultures and peoples of Asia. Art, music, and cuisine, as well as literature, are important parts of Asian cultures. Eastern philosophy and religion play a major role, with Hinduism, Taoism, Confucianism, Buddhism, Judaism, and Islam all contributing as well. Various countries have various opinions; therefore, the message and the messenger must be right. A very difficult task was being laid out for the navy. They needed unique skills, knowledge, and long-standing relationships in the community to communicate effectively with candidates and their families and to be capable of encoding and decoding messages with high-level intercultural competence.

The US Navy had to be positioned as the employer of choice for candidates and their families in high-context cultures, as much information is communicated through silence. Objections are often masked through seemingly agreeable and courteous face-saving strategies used among and between the family, prominent community members, and parents of first-generation Asian Americans. They also may attempt to use euphemisms to hide anxiety or mask disagreement. Similarly, Hispanic cultures typically avoid direct confrontation during respectful communication and may also attempt to use euphemisms to hide anxiety or mask disagreement. These communication skills were not part of the navy's repertoire and would have to be included in our training programs for recruiters.

TRADITION AS THE BASIS OF CULTURE IN THE US NAVY

The navy has a long tradition and culture rooted in hundreds of years of service. Unlike joining a corporation, when you join the navy, you are not just joining a military force. You become part of a proud tradition of core values, bravery, duty, and integrity that goes back to 1775. While ships, equipment, and technology change, many customs remain the same, including the bedrock the navy was founded on: honor, courage, and commitment. So how do you transition young people with different ethnic backgrounds and no military experience and build on the existing culture to create an environment that strengthens the corps? The navy's customs and traditions must build a bridge between young and old, past and present. It would be necessary for us to build messaging campaigns that would connect with, and appeal to, the needs, values, and high-level insights of each targeted demographic, developing the US Navy as a desirable brand for ethnic youth.

We would conduct qualitative research via interview and focus groups to develop, evaluate, and advance effective messaging. This would be a huge undertaking, essentially compelling the navy to be even more inclusive. Intercultural relationships are relatively new, as is working with others from different backgrounds, therefore management (officers and NCOs) would have to be educated as to how people from different cultures communicate with one another and how to develop an awareness of relationships within different cultures. For the recruiting campaigns, we had to develop branding and messaging strategies that would take into consideration competitive positioning to ensure that messaging resonated with the individual targeted minority audiences. We also had to develop the creative materials needed to be presented across media, including scripting, commercials, digital video, and Internet, and a social networking presence, podcasts, blogs, and events development and coordination. A priority would be to place an emphasis on tailoring creative material to reach target minority audiences.

Certain social skills to the targeted cultural audience would be needed to reduce misunderstandings:

* Dress
* Nonverbal communication
* Manners
* Ideologies
* Nationality
* Ethnicity
* Social class
* Gender

We were being charged to creatively identify, attract, recruit, and select high-quality candidates with the qualifications and competencies required to enter, and excel in, the US Navy officer corps. We knew our recruiting and selection efforts had to be based on an understanding of the cultural dynamic of individualism, collectivism, and high- and low-context cultures. The complexity of diversity within and among ethnic groups required the program design, approach, and implementation of outreach efforts to build choice and to position the US Navy as the employer of choice for candidates and their families. With that in mind, we had to develop effective messages to connect to and resonate with each distinct community in order to to attract and recruit these segments of the population. The size of this project would be enormous, especially realizing the goals in the number of recruits. It would be imperative to understand the differences among Asian cultures if the navy was to succeed in this project. Each of these cultures has its own set of values, priorities, and goals. Targeting their specific mores and identities required a clear understanding of their history and what brought them to the United States. There also needed to be a thorough understanding of how these groups communicate within their own communities, where they get their information and news, and how they make decisions. To successfully market to Asian Americans, we could not treat them as a single group.

At that point, the question needed to be asked: will diversifying have a positive effect, or is it just diversity for diversity's sake? Otherwise, what will the effect bring to the US Navy's bottom line? Asian Americans have the lowest participation of any significant minority in the American military. Per the US Census Bureau, in 2008 there were 276,000 Asian American military veterans. By contrast, there were 2.4 million single-race black veterans in the United States in 2007. There are 1.1 million Hispanic veterans of the US Armed Forces. Reaching this community would take multiple grassroots campaigns in high schools, as well as at colleges and universities. Would the return on the investment be equal to the effort? [144]

CASE STUDY: BEING AND DEFINING A TOP DIVERSITY EMPLOYER

Millington, Tennessee—The navy prides itself on being a top diversity employer and, in the past several years, has increased its efforts to improve diversity outreach, awareness, and recruiting. Diversity allows for a stronger, talented workforce, and outreach in recruiting increases the number of individuals with whom recruiters may connect to discuss navy opportunities. According to Ty Fitzgerald, PRISM Media Relations, the Navy Strategic Diversity Working Group earned the Association of Diversity Council's number-one ranking in 2013 among notable competitors such as American Airlines, which ranked number two; Boeing, number five; General Motors, number nine; and FedEx, twenty. There are approximately 323,000 sailors in today's navy. They serve around the world, each having been trained in his or her area of expertise. Many speak several languages. Many have higher education or civilian work experiences that contribute to the talent that makes our navy the best in the world. Today's sailors join from all walks of life, education, and cultural backgrounds. They bring new thoughts and ideas, working together to create a kind of synergism, said Capt. Horatio Fernandez, Navy Recruiting Command's diversity director. To create such a diverse navy, it takes a team of highly trained and motivated sailors and recruiters whose job it is to find the next generation of leaders. As competition becomes keener to fill positions in the fleet, it is important for recruiters to tap into all available communities and resources to find qualified men and women to join the navy's elite team of professionals.

Being a sailor is no regular job, and recruiting future sailors is no regular task. Recruiters face a variety of challenges and barriers that societal and cultural norms have established. It can be difficult to recruit in diverse communities. "Many diverse families struggle to accept a decision to join the Navy," said LS1 Cesar Serna, recruiter for Navy Recruiting District Jacksonville. "Reaching out to communities and helping them understand the mutual benefit to joining [the navy] is where you have to start. It's not all give, give." Awareness is one of the biggest barriers to diversity recruiting. Many individuals and families think of military service simply as boots-on-the-ground war fighting. While this is an important part of military service, most navy careers offer much more technical training and experience, said Serna. The navy's diversity outreach program helps increase awareness within communities that can develop over generations. Outreach encompasses much more than just reaching those who may be recruiting eligible. Outreach is a necessity to plant the seed years before so there is awareness of our navy and its mission, the benefits of service and learning a skill. Reaching younger audiences early helps establish a better understanding of the navy, which can then grow into a positive image in that community over time. "Diversity outreach helps generations of recruiters when outreach officers are allowed and encouraged to open doors within the local communities," said NCC William J. Riley, a navy city outreach officer for the Southeast region. "It creates personal and professional connections with key groups and figureheads who will help advance the Navy's recruiting mission." Navy Recruiting Command invests in outreach because it ultimately supports the recruiting mission. Building and maintaining relationships with key influencers across America takes time and diversity—outreach supports the longer-term view. To support the navy's recruiting mission, five diversity officers and an assistant are assigned to key cities across the United States; from east to west, outreach officers are in New York, Chicago, Atlanta, Houston, and Los Angeles. Outreach officers build and maintain relationships with key diversity organizations. They coordinate events and visits to local communities to create a navy presence. One of the key efforts they manage includes using tools like Sea Perch and science, technology, engineering, and math (STEM) displays.[145]

Sea Perch[145] is an innovative underwater robotics program that equips teachers and students with the resources they need to build an underwater remotely operated vehicle (ROV) in an in-school or out-of-school setting, according to the Sea Perch website and the Office of Naval Research. The emphasis on core STEM subjects allows students and communities to see the skills and benefits that service in the navy must offer while at the same time offering the opportunity for the navy to learn from local communities how to help with future recruiting efforts. "Our diversity outreach gives us unique views into a number of different local populations," said Lt.

Cmdr. Michael M. Kerley, the navy's city outreach officer for the Midwest, located in Chicago. "As recruiters come and go into the recruiting force, sometimes they don't know or understand these differences. We [diversity outreach] can lend our time and experience to help them fulfill their goal of being culturally educated, and a successful recruiter." In many ways, navy diversity outreach is a lot like college football outreach. Colleges frequently send their coaches and players out to local public schools as a way to get their names out there for kids at a young age. This type of outreach shows the benefits of hard work and a college education, while at the same time planting a seed for children who, in five to ten years' time, will remember the experience when it is time to apply to colleges. Navy recruiters are the coaches and team players for diversity outreach. It is important for them to understand the need for their help in outreach events. Outreach ensures the success of the recruiting mission in the future. "The long-term benefit of our program is the increased possibility of bringing Americans with various backgrounds and life experiences into naval service," said Kerley. "Our outreach efforts and local interactions may be what makes a person consider serving in the US Navy."[146]

Chapter 11

ON IMMIGRANTS—WELCOME, NOW PLEASE GO

Many Americans do not agree with bringing in immigrants to work in US companies. They feel that qualified, unemployed Americans could fill those positions and that the immigrants work for lower wages. The lower wages immigrants often accept are thought to suppress wages. Diversity brought about from immigration often challenges management. Continued use of diversity training and open communication with employees about companies' reasons for hiring immigrants may help alleviate the problem. A popular belief is that is that Americans do not want many of the manual labor and farm jobs that are available. If we accept that and agree that Americans believe they should have the better jobs, how much of these feelings have to do with prejudice and low opinions many Americans have toward immigrants. The dichotomy is that although immigrants are disproportionately represented in such high-skilled fields as medicine, physics, and computer science, the same can be said for the lower-skilled sectors, such as hotels and restaurants, domestic service, construction, and light manufacturing.[147] When many voters look at immigrants they only see the less skilled groups that they believe are threatening their livelihood.

Immigration has always been controversial in the United States. Centuries ago, Benjamin Franklin worried that too many German immigrants would swamp America's predominantly British culture. In the mid-1800s, Irish immigrants were scorned as lazy drunks, not to mention Roman Catholics. At the turn of the century a wave of "new immigrants"—Poles, Italians, and Russian Jews—were believed to be too different ever to assimilate into American life. Today the same fears are raised about immigrants from Latin America, Africa and Asia, but current critics of immigration are as wrong as their counterparts were in previous eras.[148] Immigration is not undermining the American experiment; it is an integral part of it. We are a nation of immigrants. Successive waves of immigrants have kept our country demographically young, enriched our culture, and added to our productive capacity as a nation, enhancing our influence in the world. Immigration gives the United States an economic edge in the world economy. Immigrants bring innovative ideas and entrepreneurial spirit to the US economy. They also provide business contacts to other markets, enhancing America's ability to trade and invest profitably in the global economy. They keep our economy flexible, allowing US producers to keep prices down and to respond to changing consumer demands. An authoritative study by the National Academy of Sciences (NAS) concluded that immigration delivered a "significant positive gain" to the US economy. In testimony before Congress in July 2005, former Federal Reserve Board chairman Alan Greenspan said, "I've always argued that this country has benefited immensely from the fact that we draw people from all over the world." [150]

Contrary to popular myth, immigrants do not push Americans out of jobs. Immigrants tend to fill jobs that Americans cannot or will not fill, mostly at the high and low ends of the skill spectrum. Immigrants also raise demand for goods as well as the supply.

Immigrant labor, legal and illegal, has maintained the agricultural industry for decades, and without it, food would not only be less plentiful; it might be twice as expensive. And yet so many Americans object to these immigrants, although the benefits they provide outweigh the cost. Once again, a case could be made for understanding people who have immigrated, making their lives more attractive, and providing a path to citizenship, but many anti-immigration folks have no idea what they do, and very few understand the culture of these hardworking people. This is no different from workers in a factory not understanding the need for the team contribution to manufacture their product regardless of race or ethnicity.

Yet even as immigrants continue to provide these contributions, they remain a scapegoat for disappointing economic outcomes. In the run-up to 2016 election, this became a focus of many candidates' platforms, with no explanation to the public of the positive aspects or the productivity of those at the low end of the economic spectrum. They also did not acknowledge the major contribution of immigrants to the technology and scientific fields. Historians have a concept called the scapegoating concept of history. This is the idea that people tend to look for others to blame—scapegoat—for their condition. They then attack that group even if it had little or nothing to do with their situation.[151] Late night host, comedian and satirist Stephen Colbert demonstrated the aversion of American workers to farm labor when he quit farm labor after just one day. While most actual American workers last more than a day, studies show American workers simply do not stick with farm labor. After officials in Georgia took up an anti-immigrant law, there were eleven thousand vacant farm jobs and fields left with rotten fruit and crops, and some farmers faced a labor shortage so severe they were almost forced out of business. Yet even though immigrants make up an overwhelming majority of the nation's agricultural workforce, they are not repaid for their hard work. Rather, they are subject to harsh working conditions and wage theft and are among the poorest of the working class.[152] Immigrants and their children are needed to replace baby boomers in the workplace. Baby boomers will leave 58.6 million job openings in the next two decades. Because the native-born population will not be enough to fill the number of jobs left by baby boomers, the immigrant population will be directly needed to replenish the 7.3 million workers still needed in the workforce.[153] Immigrants are not a drain on government finances. The NAS study found that the typical immigrant and his or her offspring will pay a net $80,000 more in taxes during their lifetimes than they collect in government services. For immigrants with college degrees, the net fiscal return is $198,000. It is true that low-skilled immigrants and refugees tend to use welfare more than the typical "native" household, but the 1996 Welfare Reform Act made it much more difficult for newcomers to collect welfare. As a result, immigrant use of welfare has declined in recent years, along with overall welfare rolls.[154] We have a history of bias against immigrants in this country going back to its founding. If you understand your own background, you will most likely find that your ancestors were probably Greek, Italian, Romanian, Chinese, Japanese, Sikh, Asian Indian, American Indian, Haitian, Southeast Asian (Cambodians, Vietnamese), Hispanic, or Slavic descent, are homosexual, have or had AIDS, or were part of many other groups, you have been discriminated against and stereotyped. How does it feel? Our family history makes it very difficult to build a truly productive workplace. As discussed, immigrants filled a needed place in society doing the unskilled jobs others didn't want and encouraging the derision these jobs carried with them, giving them motivation to move up and assimilate. Even though these jobs were not filled by Americans, immigrants were taking American jobs and lived through degrading and humiliating experiences based on prejudice and bigotry. Anti-immigrant groups were formed, such as the American Protective Association in the Midwest and the Immigration Restriction League in Boston. Studies and reports were commissioned to prove that Southern and Eastern Europeans were racially inferior to Northern and Western Europeans. One such study, sponsored by a nine-member Immigration Commission appointed by the US government in 1907, culminated in a forty-two-volume report to support this racist notion. Immigration policies were influenced by these reports and studies and contributed to the growing isolationist viewpoint of US government policy makers.[153] Prejudice and stereotypes go hand in hand and can allow discrimination when thought of as not favorable.

The Quota Act of 1921 put the first numerical restrictions on European immigration, followed by the Immigration Acts of 1924 and 1929. [155] The total number of immigrants permitted each year was cut by over 80 percent from the average immigration numbers at the turn of the century, and the distribution was based on the ethnic origins of the US population in 1920. As a result, 83,575 places out of a total 153,774 were assigned to Great Britain and Ireland, which provided relatively few applicants, while the smaller numbers went to countries whose immigrants were deemed undesirable based on prejudice. "Later these impersonal figures would doom Romanian, Polish, and French Jews seeking sanctuary while the English and Irish quotas lay unused." These figures were unchanged until the administration of Lyndon Johnson in the 1960s. Similarly, we have always lagged in women's rights. The Civil Rights Act of 1964 prohibited sexual discrimination regarding most employment issues, but a proposed amendment to the Constitution, the Equal Rights Amendment, to grant women equal protection under the law has yet to be ratified by the required number of states. "By the time the deadline for state ratification ended in 1982, thirty-five states had ratified the amendment, just three states short of the number needed to put the ERA into the Constitution. Since then, the ERA has been reintroduced in Congress every session. Although polls indicate that more than 90% of Americans support the ERA, Congress has not once voted on it over the past thirty years."[156] African Americans, brought to America as slaves and freed during the Civil War, have experienced discrimination ever since. Racism is still prevalent in the United States and continues to be supported by some politicians with gerrymandered voting districts, voting laws based on racial demographics, criminal laws based on the fear of blacks and black neighborhoods, and the anti-Obama movement propelled the 2016 election results where "58 percent of white voters preferred Trump, while 88 percent of black voters cast their ballot for Clinton. And perhaps more interestingly, while 94 percent of black female voters supported Clinton, 53 percent of white female voters showed a preference for Trump"[157]

There is so much more that could be discussed, but it is important to note why typical diversity programs and trainers fail in most companies. In the military, everyone is "thrown together" from day one and becomes interdependent on one another. The system works well, but prejudice and bigotry, ingrained since birth with many, often overrides the discipline of the service, and longstanding racial and religious mistrust surfaces. If one is going to be successful in building a diverse, productive, and profitable workplace, it's crucial to accept the barriers you are going to face. That is one of the many reasons we believe the training should not be mandatory. Quite frankly, very little of the time spent on understanding diversity should be canned training. It must be a condition of the job that will benefit employees by challenging them, giving them a sense of progress both financially and through advancement, creating an environment without fear, and creating trust and a feeling of community. The program begins with the interview and the job description, is detailed in the orientation, and is part and parcel of everyday life. It will not be right for everyone, but companies that understand the program will be profitable and happy businesses. More than one-third of US innovators are foreign born, which suggests highly educated immigrants might be one of America's most valuable resources. Despite making up only 13.5 percent of all US residents, 35 percent of those responsible for some of the most important innovations in America are foreign-born people, some of whom have a PhD in a STEM field, (Science, Technology, Engineering, Mathematics) according to the Washington, DC–based Information Technology and Innovation Foundation (ITIF).[158]

Had the father of the late Steve Jobs, the founder of Apple, tried to enter the country in 2017, he would have been turned away. He is Syrian. And eBay is the brain child of Pierre Omidyar, whose Iranian parents came to the U.S. from France in the 1970s. Amazon creator Jeff Bezos is the son of a Cuban father and brothers Walt and Roy Disney were born to a Canadian father. These companies and products wouldn't exist if it wasn't for these immigrants both parents and children.

SOME WELL-KNOWN IMMIGRANTS AND THEIR COMPANIES

* Sergey Brin, Russian-born American computer scientist, cofounded Google with Larry Page.
* Sun Microsystems cofounder Vinod Khosla was born in India.

* Goldman Sachs; immigrant founder: Marcus Goldman from Germany
* United Technologies; Immigrant Founder: Igor Sikorsky from Russia
* eBay founder Pierre Omidyar was born in France.
* Yahoo's cofounder Jerry Yang hails from Taiwan.
* Andrew Grove, a Hungarian immigrant, founded Intel.

DEFINITIONS

* "Foreign born" and "immigrant" are used interchangeably and refer to persons with no US citizenship at birth. This population includes naturalized citizens, lawful permanent residents, refugees and asymlees, persons on certain temporary visas, and the unauthorized.
* Latin America: Migration Policy Institute (MPI) follows the definition of Latin America as put forth by the United Nations and the US Census Bureau, which includes Central America (including Mexico), the Caribbean, and South America. For more information about geographical regions, see the US Census Bureau and UN Statistics Division.[159]

HOW MANY IMMIGRANTS RESIDE IN THE UNITED STATES?

According to estimates from the 2013 US Census Bureau's 2014 American Community Survey (ACS), the US immigrant population stood at more than 41.3 million, or 13 percent, of the total US population of 316.1 million. Between 2012 and 2013, the foreign-born population increased by about 523,000, or 1.3 percent. US immigrants and their US-born children now number approximately 84.3 million people, or 27 percent of the overall U.S. population.[160]

HISTORICAL NUMBERS AND SHARES OF IMMIGRANTS IN THE UNITED STATES [161]
Between 1860 and 1920, the immigrant share of the total population fluctuated between 13 and 15 percent, peaking at 15 percent in 1890, mainly due to high levels of European immigration.

CURRENT AND HISTORICAL NUMBERS AND SHARES
Restrictive immigration legislation in 1921 and 1924, coupled with the Great Depression and World War II, led to a sharp drop in new arrivals. Thus, the foreign-born share steadily declined between the 1930s and 1970s, reaching a record low of approximately 5 percent in 1970 (9.6 million). Since 1970, the share and number have increased rapidly, mainly because of large-scale immigration from Latin America and Asia, made possible by changes to admission rules adopted by Congress in 1965. Since 1970, the number of US immigrants has more than quadrupled as it grew from 9.6 million in 1970 to 41.3 million in 2013. [161]

SOURCE COUNTRIES
In 2013, Mexican-born immigrants accounted for approximately 28 percent of the 41.3 million foreign born in the United States, making them by far the largest immigrant group in the country. India was the second largest, closely trailed by China (including Hong Kong but not Taiwan), which both accounted for about 5

percent, while the Philippines (4 percent) was the fourth-largest sending country. Vietnam, El Salvador, Cuba, and Korea (3 percent each), as well as the Dominican Republic and Guatemala (2 percent each), complete the top ten countries of origin. Together, immigrants from these ten countries composed close to 60 percent of the US immigrant population in 2013.[162]

The predominance of immigrants from Latin American and Asian countries in the late twentieth and early twenty-first centuries starkly contrasts with the trend seen in 1960, when immigrants largely originated from Europe. Italian-born immigrants made up 13 percent of all foreign born in 1960, followed by those born in Germany and Canada (accounting for about 10 percent each). In the 1960s no single country accounted for more than 15 percent of the total immigrant population [163]

Table 1: Numerical Size and Share of the Foreign-Born Population in the United States, 1970–2013

	Size of Immigrant Population (millions)	Immigrant Share of Total U.S. Population (%)
1970	9.6	4.7
1980	14.1	6.2
1990	19.8	7.9
2000	31.1	11.1
2010	40	12.9
2013	41.3	13.1

Source: Migration Policy Institute tabulation of data from the US Census Bureau's 2010 and 2013 American Community Surveys, and 1970–2000 decennial census data.

Chapter 12

WHY THE WORD "MINORITY" LOWERS EXPECTATIONS

It is estimated that companies spend $10 billion every year on diversity initiatives, not including the time employees spend attending sessions.[164] And yet most training is not only ineffective but can be counterproductive. My company's experience has shown us that though certain basic rules of the road that satisfy EEOC regulations are necessary and have educational value, "an employer must have a certain number of employees to be covered by the laws the EEOC enforce. This number varies depending on the type of employer (for example, whether the employer is a private company, a state or local government agency, a federal agency, an employment agency, or a labor union) and the kind of discrimination alleged (for example, discrimination based on a person's race, color, religion, sex [including pregnancy, gender identity, and sexual orientation], national origin, age [forty or older], disability or genetic information)."[165]

I believe this information should be covered with all associates in the orientation programs during the initial phase of all training at a company. But to shape an inclusive organization that matches a company's goals is an entirely different project than a class describing EEOC regulations, control policies, and programs designed to limit litigation. Diversity programs should never be mandatory and should always be aimed at enhancing business goals. If associates in a business do not want to spend time to benefit the business and themselves, they most likely do not belong in the company. So many managers and CEOs waste time and money attempting to change people who either do not want to change or can't change, and both of those attitudes are unacceptable. It is time to move on and build the organization that is best for the business and benefits all associates. All qualified associates should have the opportunity to succeed, but everyone also should want to succeed according to the company's goals.

"Being able to recruit and retain a diverse group of employees has never been more important. But finding top talent is increasingly competitive, and 75 percent of prospects now evaluate likely employers and their workplaces before accepting any job offer," according to Gild.com.[166] Diversity improves the odds in recruiting talent when you have a pool of women, racial and ethnic minorities, and gay and transgender individuals in that collective. As we discussed earlier in the book, it should be no surprise that studies show diversifying the workplace helps businesses increase their market shares. In this increasingly competitive market and economy, recruiting from the largest pool of talent is not only beneficial to the company; it is essential for success.

CASE STUDY; URBAN BRANDS - ¿EN QUÉ PUEDO AYUDARLE

When I was the CEO of a retailer that had two divisions, one that marketed to African American women and the other to Latina women, we designed a plan that included customer profiles whose principal purpose was to better understand what was imperative in their lives so we could best serve them.

We could not have done this if we had not built a team that understood these customers, because many of them were the customer or lived in the communities of the customers. For sure, these were not the only necessary qualifications; they also had to be the most talented merchants, marketers, operators, financial people, distributors, planners, and as for other necessary associates we could either recruit or develop within our organization. Did we have turnover? Yes, we did. Some people were not willing to put in the work to grasp the benefit of intimately understanding the customer, and many of the programs were counterintuitive to what they had done in the past.

One incident from when I first began the job that still stands out as a lesson I have never forgotten is when I discovered that to prevent theft, we were asking customers to give us their purses and bags when they entered the stores. The stores also had cameras that recorded everyone who entered the stores and a limit of only three items allowed in the dressing rooms. Many stores had security guards, not to protect people, as most of the store associates and stores were not in any danger, but to watch the customers and discourage them from shoplifting. What a welcoming environment we were providing!

We ordered all cameras taken down, reviewed the need for guards, changed the dressing room rules, and stopped the policy of taking purses and bags. Our loss prevention department initially refused to do what I asked, as did some of the senior store personnel. There were also many in the company who thought I had lost my mind but kept their opinions to themselves. I finally had to order that all cameras be express shipped to my office by a certain date and the store number be attached to each. Within a week, I had hundreds of cameras spilling out of my office, setting exactly the example I wanted for the associates. There were a few missing, as some just thought I was dead wrong. Those associates were dismissed—as was the VP of loss prevention. They were never going to be customer friendly, as they were biased toward the customer. Trusting the store managers and the customers paid off; our loss was reduced by two percent as word got out, and both the staff and customers took pride and ownership in "their" store and ensured they were friendly and profitable. A bonus program was then devised, combining sales and profitability, and everyone shared in the bottom line.

There is another program I recommend to companies to ensure everyone is on the same page. As CEO, I would spend one full day every month with all the new hires and, along with other senior managers, present an orientation that defined the business, its goals, and the means for each person to achieve those goals. Every new hire gathered for these meetings regardless of position: warehouse, accounting, buyers, store personnel, and executives. This meant every associate received the same message. Each session also included veteran associates so everyone in the company got the message and better understood the direction of the company.

Diversity in the work environment must promote acceptance, respect, and teamwork. Acceptance of individual differences is essential in creating a happy and productive work environment. Acceptance leads to respect and, ultimately opportunity [167]

As discussed, many times in this book, EEOC compliance is not a substitute for a productive and profitable diverse workplace. One must realize and identify any individual issues such as prejudice, racism, gender, harassment, and other forms of discrimination existing in the business that need to be eliminated and will require management guidance and a zero-tolerance policy. To best take the temperature of an organization, in-house expertise or outsourced professionals should perform an HR audit to help identify the strengths and weaknesses of the employment practices and culture of the business.

Two of the oldest and most persistent issues in a workplace are "men versus women" and harassment. Though not always connected, harassment can never be tolerated. Harassment has often been ignored or overlooked due to historical experiences and this cannot be tolerated. One must understand that any comment can be considered harassment if any racial, sexual, or biased implication is included, even in statements one might think positive, such as, "I think black women are beautiful."

"Workplace harassment is alleged in approximately 30 percent of all charges filed with the US Equal Employment Opportunity Commission (EEOC)," according to EEOC Chair Jenny R. Yang.[168] Harassment in the workplace probably occurs more often than is reported and continues to be the number-one negative issue facing a company. Sexual harassment in the workplace shows a disrespect for coworkers and is detrimental to the individual being harassed, as well as the entire community. A strong diversity program has zero tolerance for sexual harassment. A business that is lax concerning sexual behavior most likely lacks the discipline to be effective and successful.

The best prevention is to hire the right people and ask the right questions. When designing your diversity strategic plan interview, include questions that relate to the needs of your workplace and give you the best chance to hire the right people, questions concerning inclusion, cultural competencies, environment, stereotyping, communication techniques, understanding other cultures, languages spoken, resolving conflicts, overcoming obstacles, and performance standards, as well as asking why the candidate desires to work in a diverse business.

DIVERSITY FOR FUN AND PROFIT

CASE STUDY: ROGER AILES AND SEXUAL HARASSMENT – STILL A MAJOR WORKPLACE CHALLENGE

Roger Ailes had a long and successful career as an Emmy-winning TV producer (*The Mike Douglas Show*), Richard Nixon's executive producer for television, a political consultant for George H. W. Bush, and an adviser after 9/11 to President George W. Bush. Beginning in 1968 with the founding of his consulting firm, Ailes Communication, he consulted for a number of politicians and businesses and produced two successful Broadway plays.[169] His success as a political consultant led in 1984 to the presidential campaign of Ronald Reagan. It is widely believed that Ailes's coaching of Reagan was the deciding factor that allowed Reagan to win the second presidential debate with Walter Mondale. In 1988, Ailes wrote a book with longtime aide Jon Kraushar, called *You Are the Message: Secrets of the Master Communicators*, in which he discusses some of his philosophies and strategies for successful performance in the public eye.[170] In 1993, Roger Ailes was named president of CNBC. When he left CNBC, he was hired by Rupert Murdoch to create the now-famous Fox News Channel for Murdoch's News Corporation. Fox News quickly became the most-watched cable news network in the United States. On October 7, 1996, Ailes became the founding CEO of Fox News and was named chairman of the Fox Television Stations Group on August 15, 2005. Ailes also was chairman of several of parent company, 20th Century Fox entities, earning well over $25 million per year.[171] Roger Ailes, by any measure, was extremely successful; many believed him to be the most powerful man in television news or television itself. And now his reputation and career has been destroyed, because he sexually harassed women his entire career and despite all his success the headline of his front-page obituary called out "harasser".

This account serves as a lesson and demonstrates how a lack of understanding the need for diversity in any business or in one's personal life can ruin a reputation earned over a lifetime. In Roger Ailes's case, he never understood this, as he was a serial harasser with a record of misogyny and sexual harassment going back decades, and this culture permeated every company and relationship Mr. Ailes was in or worked for. For all his accomplishments, he will be remembered for being a harasser, and those men who worked for him and who certainly were aware of the culture and did nothing will carry the same stigma with them wherever they go. Sexual harassment was pervasive at Fox. Dozens of women report it was a "locker room" environment, and the lawsuits will continue for years. There will be tens of millions of dollars paid to the claimants, which Fox's parent company can afford but most businesses could not. Not only is sexual harassment contemptible and morally wrong, it is bad business.

Despite many accounts such as this, sexual harassment continues to be a major problem in the workplace, creating a hostile environment for women, causing many to leave. I have found, in our diversity consultancy, that many in top management do not attend the training sessions and have no real idea what sexual harassment constitutes. One out of three women report they have experienced harassment in the workplace.[172] In some cases, a woman can risk losing her job or a promotion. But it also creates an environment where women are stereotyped as sexual objects. It can cost companies millions in lawsuits. In our opinion, it is not different from sexual assault, and we believe it should be criminalized. There is absolutely no place in business or anywhere for this behavior. Serious harassment cannot be trained out, and it should not be attempted. The individual should be fired for cause. Steps can be taken to prevent unintentional sexual harassment, and training should be given to every employee as part of the company orientation.

Building a diverse workforce for the future requires a company culture and a CEO who understands the needs of a diverse workforce for a "place that is comfortable, safe, supportive and considerate to their needs, values and concerns."[173] To effectively reach, serve, and retain customers in an increasingly competitive environment, businesses must closely examine and reevaluate their marketing strategies. Managers should be sure that those within the company share some of the same attributes as the customer. Management teams at many businesses may strive to mirror the population, but rarely do they succeed. A truly diverse management team is a rare thing indeed. Often it appears to be diverse but in practice it is not. It is as if the placement of certain employees allows there to be a perception of a diverse management group, but in the end the decision makers all look the same.

There are so many convenient misconceptions about building and maintaining a diverse workforce that many of those in hiring positions believe it is easier to just not try that hard. The motivation behind creating a diverse workforce must be more than just trying to do the right thing. Those responsible for hiring need to really understand why they are trying to attract and retain a diverse pool of employees and why it can change how customers view the company and how the company works.

Americans are generally not comfortable with the unfamiliar, and for many, minorities or people who don't look or act as they do are mysterious and even a little scary. In some cases, employees have expressed outright fear over working with someone who looks and sounds different from other coworkers. In its most basic form, it is commonly accepted that prejudice has different points of origin, chief among them being fear. The first is the expectation that the unfamiliar might cause harm. Next is the perception that another person's different world view will create conflict and challenges, and the presumption that interaction will lead to discomfort or embarrassment, rejection, or ridicule. Obviously, before a truly diverse workforce can be cohesive, productive, and profitable, these misconceptions must be dispelled and cast aside. This cannot be accomplished through a half-day mandatory sensitivity training program that no one wants to attend. There are very few programs to create a diverse workplace that work and even fewer success stories of companies that have mastered the concept of finding and hiring the best people for the job regardless of what they look like. But those companies share a rare quality: cohesiveness, profitability, and general satisfaction among employees. The big question is, how do you do that for your company?

Whether creating a diverse workplace is a moral obligation, a method to understand and therefore reach a more diverse customer pool, or a public relations tool to make a company look good, it is a good business practice. The problem with diversity programming and training, as it exists today, is that it doesn't really work. It makes management happy to know that the effort is being made and that the company annual report lists diversity training as a priority. The human resources department includes a designated diversity manager position, employees are required to attend training sessions that teach them how to behave so no one sues, and awards are handed out to the companies that spend the most on their diversity programming.

What does a company need to do to create and administer an effective meaningful effort to bring diversity to the workplace? The first thing that needs to be understood is that it doesn't mean poring over training manuals. It doesn't mean winning the most diversity awards. It also doesn't mean filling slots based on how many members of each ethnic or racial group a company feels it needs to have. It's a new way of considering what an effective workforce looks like, how it interacts, and how it can benefit profitability and enhance a corporate image. ***It is Diversity for Fun and Profit***

INSPIRATION

I recently read an interview with John Leguizamo entitled "The First Time I Faced a Hostile Audience (Kid)" [174] He was describing his early years in the theater and the difficulty getting acting jobs that paid the rent. Leguizamo is quoted as saying "that the only gig I could get was a diverse children's troupe that was hiring my flavor." The troupe, Off Center Theater was mostly Latin and black and travelled around New York City performing at schools mostly in Latin and black areas. The actors knew these kids, they had been them and knew they would rather be somewhere else, hence the hostile audiences. But once they began changing the plays so the kids could relate and they realized "how hungry my young Latin people were to be entertained by their own". At the schools, the actors would update the classics; "We did "Little Red Riding Hood" where she was a fine black girl and suddenly the Big Bad Wolf would start beat boxing."[175] They added Stevie Wonder and Michael Jackson impressions and Frankenstein's monster became a break-dancer. What John and his troupe discovered that what they saw in movies and TV was not the real world these students lived in. By entertaining them in their "lingo" and mannerisms their culture was validated and showed they were "important and cool". Of all the examples in this book relating to "knowing your customer" this may be the most perfect illustration.

ADDENDUM

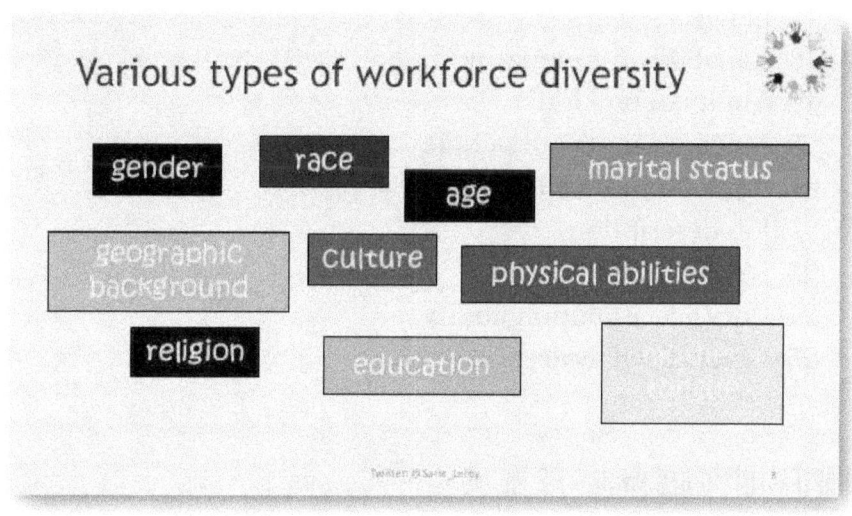

TWENTY-FIVE EXAMPLES OF DIVERSITY IN THE WORKPLACE

1. Age
2. Gender
3. Race and ethnicity
4. Education
5. Physical appearance
6. Physical ability
7. Culture
8. Problem-solving ability
9. Critical thinking ability
10. Team building ability
11. Communication ability
12. Income
13. Music enjoyed
14. Type of books read
15. TV shows enjoyed

16. Experiences when being raised
17. Language
18. Capability for empathy
19. Ability to be kind
20. Ability to motivate people
21. Ability to work with others
22. Job description
23. Listening ability
24. Conflict resolution ability
25. Level of self-awareness

CHAPTER: 1 IN THE BEGINNING – ME, ME, ME

CHAPTER 2: KUMBAYA; DEVOTIONS AT WORK

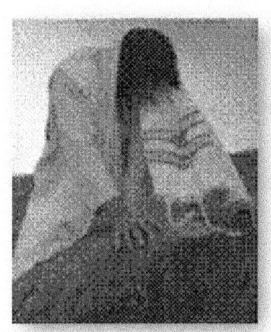

CHAPTER 3: TIMES ARE CHANGING
The Importance of Community in Building a Diverse Workforce

CHAPTER 4: WE CAN'T FIND ANY OF THOSE
No, 'Hispanic' And 'Latino' Are Not the Same Thing

Yes, **we are here!**

CHAPTER 5: WHY CREATE A DIVERSE WORKPLACE

CHAPTER 6: THE BENEFITS OF DIVERSE AGES AND GENDERS IN THE WORKPLACE

Tapping the Full Potential of diversity in the workplace:
culture, age, gender & disability aspect

CHAPTER 7: THE ABCS OF LGBT

The 25 Best Companies for LGBT Employees; Glassdoor.com

1. Bain & Company
2. Orbitz Worldwide
3. Google
4. McKinsey & Company
5. Boston Consulting Group
6. NIKE
7. Intuit
8. Genentech
9. Chevron
10. Apple
11. Ford Motor
12. Hyatt
13. eBay

14. Bristol-Myers Squibb
15. Disney
16. Monsanto & Company
17. Johnson & Johnson
18. Sony Pictures Entertainment
19. Unilever
20. Microsoft
21. A.T. Kearney
22. Yahoo
23. GlaxoSmithKline
24. Cisco Systems
25. General Mills

CHAPTER: 8 UNDERSTANDING THE DIVERSE CUSTOMER—INCLUSION AS A DRIVER OF BUSINESS

Dr. Dorothy Height was a leader of the African American and women's rights movements and was considered both the Grande dame of the civil rights era and its unsung heroine. Dr. Dorothy Height, was an Advisory Board member and mentor to ESA Associates, LLC.

Dr. Height had a career in civil rights that spanned nearly eighty years, from anti-lynching protests in the early 1930s to the inauguration of President Obama in 2009. That the American social landscape looks as it does today is due in no small part to her work. Dr. Height was president of the National Council of Negro Women from 1957 to 1997, overseeing a range of programs on issues like voting rights, poverty, and in later years AIDS. A longtime executive of the YWCA, she presided over the integration of its facilities nationwide in the 1940s. With Gloria Steinem, Shirley Chisholm,

Betty Friedan, and others, she helped found the National Women's Political Caucus in 1971. Over the decades, she advised a string of American presidents on civil rights. If Ms. Height was less well known than her contemporaries in either the civil rights or the women's movement, it is perhaps because she was doubly marginalized, pushed offstage by women's groups because of her race and by black groups because of her sex. Throughout her career, she responded quietly but firmly, working with a characteristic mix of limitless energy and steely gentility to ally the two movements in the fight for social justice. As a result, Ms. Height is widely credited as the first person in the modern civil rights era to treat the problems of equality for women and equality for African Americans as a seamless whole, merging concerns that had been largely historically separate. The recipient of the Presidential Medal of Freedom and other prestigious awards, Ms. Height was accorded a place of honor on the dais on January 20, 2009, when Mr. Obama took the oath of office as the nation's forty-fourth president. Over the years, historians have made much of the so-called Big Six who led the civil rights movement: The Reverend Dr. Martin Luther King Jr., James Farmer, John Lewis, A. Philip Randolph, Roy Wilkins, and Whitney M. Young Jr. Ms. Height, the only woman to work regularly alongside them on projects of national significance, was very much the unheralded seventh, the leader who was cropped out, figuratively and often literally, of images of the era. In 1963, for instance, Ms. Height sat on the platform an arm's length from Dr. King as he delivered his epochal "I Have a Dream" speech at the March on Washington. She was one of the march's chief organizers and a prizewinning orator herself. Yet she was not asked to speak, although many other black leaders—all men—addressed the crowd that day. Ms. Height recounted the incident in her memoir, Open Wide the Freedom Gates (Public Affairs), 2003). Reviewing the memoir, the New York Times Book Review called it "a poignant short course in a century of African American history." Besides the

Presidential Medal of Freedom, awarded by President Bill Clinton in 1994, Ms. Height's many honors include the Congressional Gold Medal, awarded by President George W. Bush in 2004. The two medals are the country's highest civilian awards. Ms. Height received three dozen honorary doctorates from institutions, including Tuskegee, Harvard, and Princeton Universities. But there was one academic honor—the equivalent of a bachelor's degree—that resonated more strongly than all the rest: in 2004, seventy-five years after turning her away, Barnard College designated Ms. Height an honorary graduate.

CHAPTER 9: UNDERSTANDING THE DIVERSE CUSTOMER—INCLUSION AS A DRIVER OF BUSINESS

Customer Diversity: Providing Great Customer Experience Across Cultures

Know your customers and seek out culture-specific knowledge

CHAPTER 10: THE AMERICAN WAY, THE CORPORATE WAY, THE POLITICAL WAY
The American Way

Diversity Imagine all the People

The Corporate Way
Invest in women and minority-led companies

The Political Way
The U.S. Still Has a Long Way to Go to Achieve True Diversity in Politics

CHAPTER 11: AYE-AYE, SIR...ER, MA'AM – THE ELEMENTS FOR BUILDING A DIVERSE WORKFORCE AND CULTURE

America's Navy is a place where men and women of every cultural background proudly take the lead, bringing their different skills, backgrounds and talents to bear every day, creating an environment of excellence

Women's History Month:
U.S. Navy Women Trailblazers

The African American Experience
in the U.S. Navy

CHAPTER 12: ON IMMIGRANTS—WELCOME, NOW PLEASE GO

The Irish

The Jews

The Syrians

The Italians

ETHAN S. SHAPIRO

CHAPTER 13: WHY THE WORD "MINORITY" LOWERS EXPECTATIONS

We Should Celebrate American Minorities

SONGS

* Ah! Sweet Mystery of Life
* 1910 - m. Victor Herbert (1859-1924), w. Rida Johnson Young (1875-1926) P - Naughty Marietta
* Just as Well as He, Lyrics: Adella Hunt Logan, Music: to the tune of "Coming through the Rye"- Year: 1912
* Masculine Women! Feminine Men! - Lyrics: Edgar Leslie, Music: James V. Monaco
* Kumbaya" or "Kumbaya" or "Cumbaya" (Gullah, "come by here"—"kum ba yah") is a spiritual song first recorded in the 1920s
* Somewhere over the Rainbow," from The Wizard of Oz, lyrics by E. Y. Harburg, music by Harold Arlen, performed by Judy Garland, 1939. Published by © Sony/ATV Music Publishing LLC
* 9 to 5, Working 9 to 5"; Songwriters, Florrie Palmer and Dolly Parton, published by © Warner/Chappell Music, Inc., Sony/ATV Music Publishing LLC, Performed by Dolly Parton - Released: 1980
* This Land Is Your Land" Song by Woody Guthrie Published 1945 Recorded 1944 Writer(s) Woody Guthrie

ENDNOTES

1. Kaylene C. Williams and Robert A. Page, *Journal of Behavioral Studies in Business*, http://www.aabri.com/manuscripts/10575.pdf./

2. *The Psychology of Diversity: Beyond Prejudice and Racism*, by James M. Jones, John F. Dovidio, and Deborah L. Vietze, Wiley-Blackwell, 2014.

3. "How to Fix Politics" by David Brooks, *New York Times*, April 12, 2016.

4. For the first half of the century, American universities had Jew quotas, which limited the intake of Jewish students to no more than 10 percent

5. *Schwartze* is a term used by some Jewish people to refer to a black person; *shiksa* is a non- Jewish (Gentile) girl or woman; *shagetz* is a non-Jewish (Gentile) male; *goy* is a term used by a Jew to refer to someone who is not Jewish; *yutzi* refers to something or someone that is stupid; and *mensch* is a good or important person, almost always Jewish unless named Roosevelt.

6. "Historical Development of Institutional Racism: A Working Paper," by Robette Ann Dias, Crossroads Antiracism Organizing & Training, May 2006, updated and revised May 2013, http://www.crossroadsantiracism.org/

7. "Turning Around Polarized Mindsets in Workplace Mediations—Conclusion," by Jack Hamilton and Elisabeth Seaman, Mediate.com, http://www.mediate.com/articles/workplace.cfm/ .

8. "Hostile Work Environments—Escalating Conflict and What You Can Do about It," by Gayle Oudeh and Nabil Oudeh, The Free Conflict Help Center, http://conflict911.com/guestconflict/nabil.htm/

9. "Kumbaya" or "Kumbayah" or "Cumbaya" (Gullah, "come by here"—"kum ba yah") is a spiritual song first recorded in the 1920s. It became a standard campfire song in Scouting and summer camps and enjoyed broader popularity during the folk revival of the 1950s and 1960s. The song was originally a simple appeal to God to come and help those in need. The two earliest versions whose years of origin are known for certain were both collected in 1926, and both reside in the Library's American Folklife.

10. Federal Laws Prohibiting Job Discrimination Questions and Answers; Federal Equal Employment Opportunity (EEO) Laws - https://www.eeoc.gov/facts/qanda.html/

11. National Archives, EEOC Terminology; https://www.archives.gov/eeo/terminology.html/

12. Information Age; The business of diversity: how a diverse workforce makes money, 1/30/17- http://www.information-age.com/business-diversity-diverse-workforce-makes-money-123464193//

13. EEOC Budget; https://www.eeoc.gov/eeoc/plan/archives/budgets/eeocbudgets/

14. Audio English.org; Meaning of Minority - http://www.audio-english.org/dictionary/minority.htm/

15. EEOC Terminology; National Archives Equal Employment Opportunity Program

16. Ethnic and Racial Disparities in Education: Psychology's Contributions to Understanding and Reducing Disparities; A Report of the APA Presidential Task Force on Educational Disparities, August 3, 2012 https://www.apa.org/ed/resources/racial-disparities.pdf/

17. Continuity and Evolution of Animals by N.S. Sharma; Chapter 7, Human Evolution Page 243

18. EEOC Compliance Manual; Directives Transmittal - Number 915.003 EEOC

19. A Religious Studies Approach to Questions about Religious Diversity by Ian S. Markham The Oxford Handbook of Religious Diversity; Edited by Chad Meister, Print Publication Date: Dec 2010

20. Top 50 Companies for Diverse Managers to Work; Diversity MBA Magazine – http://diversitymbamagazine.com/50-out-front-companies-for-diverse-managers-to-work/

21. Diversity is a Way of Life at Wal-Mart - http://corporate.walmart.com/_news_/news-archive/2006/03/03/diversityisawayoflifeatwalmart/

22. The Gateway Bank America/Merrill Lynch - http://thegatewayonline.com/internships/investment-banking/bank-of-america-merrill-lynch-associate-internship-programme-2014/

23. Inclusion and Diversity; Denise Young Smith; Vice President of Worldwide Human Resources- http://www.apple.com/diversity/

24. US News & World Report, https://www.usnews.com/news/articles/2015/07/06/its-official-the-us-is-becoming-a-minority-majority-nation/

25. https://www.usnews.com /itsofficialtheusisbecomingaminoritymajoritynationvoting/ US Census Bureau/

26. https://www.census.gov/content/dam/Census/library/publications//.../p25-1143.pdf

27. May 5, 2016 Ridley's Believe It or Not Cinco de Mayo, Michael P. Ridley aka the Alaskan poet, www.alaskanpoet.blogspot.com

28. Hispanic Population Growth; https://www.census.gov/newsroom /releases/archives/2010 _census/cb11-cn125

29. Black-White Conflict Isn't Society's Largest, Pew Research Center- http://www.pewsocialtrends.org/2009/09/24/black-white-conflict-isnt-societys-largest/

30. Racial and Ethnic Diversity in the United States, Boundless.com-https://www.boundless.com/political-science/textbooks/boundless-political-science-textbook/american-politics-1/who-is-american-21/racial-and-ethnic-diversity-in-the-united-states-123-11224/

31. Population Projections of the United States by Age, Sex, Race, and Hispanic Origin: 1995 to 2050, https://www.census.gov/prod/1/pop/p25-1130.pdf/

32. Diversity at Amazon; http://www.careerbuilder.com/company/amazon/

33. The Downside of Diversity by Michael Jonas, The Boston Globe, Boston.com news - http://archive.boston.com/news/globe/ideas/articles/2007/08/05/the_downside_of_diversity/

34. Info Please, Women by the Numbers-From the U.S. Census Bureau http://www.infoplease.com/spot/women census1.htm/

35. AAUW; The Truth about the Gender Pay Gap - The Women's Debate Apr 3, 2016

36. Institute for women's Policy Research - Pay Equity & Discrimination, Racial & Ethnic Inequality; The Gender Wage Gap by Occupation 2015 and by Race and Ethnicity, April 11, 2016- http://http//www.womensdebate.org/%20pdf%20/%20Gender-Pay-Gap-AAUW.pdf/

37. Closing the Gender Wage Gap Would Cut Women's Poverty Rate in Half by Bryce Covert, Economic Editor at Think Progress - https://thinkprogress.org/closing-the-gender-wage-gap-would-cut-womens-poverty-rate-in-half-85bb61af8530#.pwvwkvbg/

38. How the Wage Gap Hurts Women and Families - July 2015; National Women's Law Center; https://nwlc.org/wp-content/

uploads/2015/08/7.8.15howthewagegaphurtswomenandfamilies.pdf

39. Cornel University ILR School - Managing Diversity and Glass Ceiling Initiatives as National Economic Imperatives Taylor Cox Jr. United States Glass Ceiling Commission Carol Smolinski United States Glass Ceiling Commission

40. Nielson; U.S Women Control the Purse Strings Consumer | 04-02-2013, http://www.nielsen.com/us/en/insights/news/2013/u-s--women-control-the-purse-strings.html/

40a http://www.nielsen.com/us/en/insights/news/2013/u-s--women-control-the-purse-strings.html/

41. Adella Hunt Logan b. 1863; d. 12 December 1915), educator. Born in Sparta, Georgia, Hunt was the daughter of a free mulatto woman and a white planter—the fourth of eight children. In 1883 Adella taught at the American Missionary School before joining Booker T. Washington and Olivia Davidson at the Tuskegee Institute. She taught English and Social Sciences and served as Tuskegee's first librarian

42. The Sociology of Discrimination: Racial Discrimination in Employment, Housing, Credit, and Consumer Markets Devah Pager and Hana Shepherd- https://www.ncbi.nlm.nih.gov/pmc/articles/PMC2915460/

43. Minorities, International Encyclopedia of Social Sciences; http://www.encyclopedia.com/philosophy-and-religion/

other-religious-beliefs-and-general-terms/miscellaneous-religion/minorities/

44. CNN Politics, DHS Secretary Jeh Johnson backs local law enforcement, says tactics should be reviewed by Daniella Diaz, CNN July 10, 2016

45. The McGill Daily; The oppressive power of language, http://www.mcgilldaily.com/2011/03/

46. Racial and Ethnic Groups, Fourteenth Edition by Richard T. Schaefer - Pearson Education Limited 2015

47. Spicer Defends the Cabinets Diversity, The Washington Post – 2/20/17 - https://www.washingtonpost.com/

48. BEST PRACTICES IN ACHIEVING WORKFORCE DIVERSITY; U.S. DEPARTMENT OF COMMERCE https://govinfo.library.unt.edu/npr/library/workforce-diversity.pdf/

49. Researched using The Diversity Task Force of the American Library Association Staff Diversity and Inclusion Plan Bibliography http://www.ala.org/offices/sites/ala.org.offices/files/content/diversity/ALADiversityActionandInclusionPlan.pdf

50. The Role of Finance in the Strategic-Planning and Decision-Making Process, Global Supply Chain Review - http://www.gscreview.com/feb10rolestrategicplanningphp

51. Meliorate, what is the Relationship Between Corporate Culture and Strategy? by Torben Rick | June 7, 2013 | Corporate Culture, Strategy - https://www.torbenrick.eu/blog/strategy/relationship-between-culture-and-strategy/

52. Revitalizing U.S. Economic Growth in the 21st Century," - by Jerry W. Thomas, https://www.decisionanalyst.com/whitepapers/economicgrowth/

53. Forbes; Top 10 Reasons Diversity Is Good for The Boardroom by Mike Myatt

54. Bridging the communication gap between Generation Y and the Baby Boomer generation by Elza Venter http://www.tandfonline.com/ doi/full/10.1080/02673843.2016.1267022

55. Recruiting Brief; The Benefits of Hiring a Multigenerational Workforce, 11/3/2015-http://www.recruitingbrief.com%20%20%20benefits/employer-branding/survey/

56. Mentor-Protege Relationships in the Age-diverse Workplace; Designing Mentoring Programs that Work- http://singlepoint.com/mentoring-at-work//

57. CNBC, the 10 global companies trying to lead on diversity: Study by Eric Rosenbaum 24 Apr 2015 http://www.cnbc.com/2015/04/24/the-10-global-companies-trying-to-lead-on-diversity:-study.html/

58. Havas PR North America, Marian Salzman, http://havaspr.com/?page_id=276/

59. Winning the workplace generation game; From THE ECONOMIST, Published 9/30/13

60. The Economist, Generations in the workplace; Winning the generation game- 9/26/13, http://www.economist.com/news/business/

61. What is Creativity? - Creativity at Work, http://www.creativityatwork.com/2014/02/17/what-is-creativity/

62. Want a Team to be Creative? Make it Diverse by Beth Comstock; Harvard Business Review – 5/11/12 https://hbr.org/2012/05/want-a-team-to-be-creative-mak/

63. Gender Diversity, Hunt, Layton, Prince (January 2015). "Why diversity matters.". McKinsey.

64. "Men vs. Women,": by Why the work divide matters, by Katherine Crowley and Kathi Elster; Special to Upstart Business Journal - 1/10/13 - http://www.ibtimes.com/patricia-arquette-oscars-acceptance-speech-2015-boyhood-winner-talks-womens-rights-1824474.

65. What's Holding Women Back? The Economist; http://www.economist.com/blogs

66. Business Insider; The 25 Best Companies for LGBT Employees by Jacquelyn Smith – 3/6/14 - http://www.businessinsider.com/best-companies-for-lgbt-employees-2014-3

67. The Williams Institute; The Business Impact of LGBT-Supportive Workplace Policies M.V. Lee Badgett, Laura E.

Durso, Angeliki Kastanis & Christy Mallory- https://williamsinstitute.law.ucla.edu/wp- Business-Impact-of-LGBT-Policies-May-2013.pdf/

68. Protest Song: Masculine Women! Feminine Men! Lyrics: Edgar Leslie, Music: James V. Monaco 1925

69. International Competitiveness in and the New Economy, the role of Diversity and Equality; GLEN - http://www.glen.ie/attachments/International_Competitiveness.PDF/

70. CNN Money; Still missing: Female business leaders by Matt Egan - http://investing/female-ceo- pipeline-leadership/%20 http://money.cnn.com/2015/03/24//

71. Stonewall. https://www.staffs.ac.uk/assets/Stonewall%20-%20Employment%20regulations%20- 20guidelines%20for%20employerstcm44-21515.pdf

72. Investopedia; The 2007-08 Financial Crisis in Review by Manoj Singh- http://www.investopedia.com/articles/

73. Center for American Progress, Gay and Transgender People Face High Rates of Workplace Discrimination and Harassment by Crosby Burns and Jeff Krehely; https://www.americanprogress.org/issues/lgbt/news/2011/06/02/9872/

74. "Somewhere over the Rainbow," from The Wizard of Oz, lyrics by E. Y. Harburg, music by Harold Arlen, performed by Judy Garland, 1939. Published by © Sony/ATV Music

Publishing LLC Song Discussions is protected by U.S. Patent 9401941. Other patents pending

75. KPMG; Sexual Orientation and Gender Diversity in the Workplace, https://issuu.com/aconhealth/docs/pid/ sexual orientationhandbook//

76. Glen -Gay & Lesbian Equality Network; Diversity Champions, Building the Business Case for Diversity, http://www.diversitychampions.ie/attachments/14e91ce1-ab77-47c9-a3e2-6f43c31616b9/

77. Glaad; The Value of LGBT Equality in the Workplace by Michaela Krejcova, 2/26/15 - http://www.glaad.org%20%20/blog/value-lgbt-equality-workplace/

78. US News; Gay Couples Increase in Red and Blue States Alike There are more same-sex couples nationwide. by Danielle Kurtzleben, Staff Writer - https://www.usnews.com/news/articles/2011/09/28/gay-couples-increase-in-red-and-blue-states-alike/

79. Business Case for Inclusion and Engagement, by Marcus Robinson, Charles Pfeffer, and Joan Buccigrossi, Rochester, NY

80. The Guardian; Sexuality, Lord Browne: 'I thought being gay was basically wrong' - https://www.theguardian.com/society/2014/may/24/lord-browne-thought-being-gay-wrong-interview-bp-boss- homophobia

81. Bloomberg Technology; Tim Cook Speaks Up, by Timothy Donald Cook 10/30/14 - https://www.bloomberg.com/news/articles/2014-10-30/tim-cook-speaks-up/

82. Human Rights Campaign; Corporate Equality Index Criteria 2017- Updated on 02/01/2017 - http://www.hrc.org/%20%20%20resources/2016-Corporate-Equality-Index-Criteria/

83. Human Rights Campaign; HRC Takes Action Against Saks Fifth Avenue for Undermining LGBT Equality by Stephen Peters 1/8/15- http://www.hrc.org/blog?gclid=CJym2J_rkNQCFcS6wAodV-QHhw/

84. Glaad; The Value of LGBT Equality in the Workplace- Benefits for Business 2/26/15, http://www.glaad.org/blog/ The Business Case for Diversity; http://www.theiilp.com/resources/Documents/IILPBusinessCaseforDiversity.pdf/

85. 9 to 5, Working 9 to 5"; Songwriters, Florrie Palmer and Dolly Parton, published by © Warner/Chappell Music, Inc., Sony/ATV Music Publishing LLC, Performed by Dolly Parton - Released: 1980

86. Cnet.com; Tech leaders are using their voices, influence to speak out on social, political issues, by Terry Collins 4/5/15- https://www.cnet.com/news//

87. FTI Consulting Projects U.S. Online Retail Sales to Approach $440 Billion in 2017, Online Market Share Expected to Nearly Double by 2026

88. Social Media Today; 24 Statistics That Show Social Media Is the Future of Customer Service by Mike Scheinder, 11/11/15

89. Appleinsider; Apple highlights LGBT content with special curated App Store section/ 6/25/15 - http://appleinsider.com/articles/15/06/25/apple-honors-lgbt-movement-with-special-curated-app-store-section/

90. Business, Inc.; How Companies Are Changing Their Culture to Attract (And Retain) Millennials, https://www.business.com/articles/how-are-companies-changing-their-culture-to-attract-and-retain-millennials/

91. Business, Inc; How to Lose a Millennial in 10 Days by Matthews Derek 2/22/17, https://www.business.com/articles/how-to-lose-a-millenial-in-10-days/

92. UNC, Keenan -Flagler Business School - http://www.kenan-flagler.unc.edu/404.html/

93. The Huffington Post, How to Work Successfully with A Younger Boss by Paul Bernard, 05/15/2013- http://www.huffingtonpost.com/paul-bernard/younger-boss-how-to-work-successfully_b_3266922.html/

94. Accommodating Religious Diversity in the Workplace, A survey Report by the Society for Human Resource Management (SHRM) - http://www.diversityinc.com/medialib/uploads/2011/12/08625ReligionSR FinalLowRez.pdf/

95. Interfaith Center of Greater Philadelphia; Beyond Accommodation: Religious Diversity in the Workplace- http://www.interfaithcenterpa.org/religious-diversity-in-the-workplace/

96. Harvard Business Review, The New Path To the C-Suite by Boris Groysberg, L. Kevin Kelly, and Bryan MacDonald https://hbr.org/ 2011/03/the-new- path-to-the-c-suite/

97. The Balance.com; Cultural Diversity in the Work Place; How Diversity at Work Makes More Money for You- https://www.thebalance.com/cultural-diversity-330620/

98. Euromonitor; Cultural Diversity and its Impact on Global Consumer Markets, http://www.euromonitor.com/cultural-diversity-and-its-impact-on-global-consumer-markets/report/

99. Pew Research Center, U.S. Hispanic and Asian populations growing, but for different reasons by Anna Brown- http://www.pewresearch.org/fact-tank/

100. Migration Policy Institute (MPI), Frequently Requested Statistics on Immigrants and Immigration in the United States by Jie Zong and Jeanne Batalova

101. Migration Policy Institute (MPI), Frequently Requested Statistics Frequently Requested Statistics on Immigrants and Immigration in the United States

102. Migration Policy Institute (MPI), Frequently Requested Statistics Frequently Requested Statistics on Immigrants and Immigration in the United States

103. The Chicago Urban League; The African-American Consumer; Nielson & Essence - http://www.thechicagourbanleague.org/cms/lib07/IL07000264/Centricity/Domain/76/nieslen-essence-2014-african-american-consumer-report-Sept-2014.pdf/

104. Chicago Defender, What's in Your Wallet? Supporting Black-Owned Business by Mary L. Datcher, Chicago Defender Sr. Staff Writer - https://chicagodefender.com/2016/12/20/whats-in-your-wallet-supporting-black-owned-business//

105. Lyrics written 1831 by Samuel Francis Smith. The melody is the same as that of the national anthem of the United Kingdom, "God Save the Queen", arranged by Thomas Arne.

106. The Doctrine of Discovery, 1493; https://www.gilderlehrman.org/history-by-era/imperial-rivalries/resources/doctrine-discovery-1493/

107. National Center for Research in Vocational Education (NCRVE), http://ncrve.berkeley.edu/

108. Dimensions of Racism; the Office of the United Nations High Commissioner for Human Rights OHCHR)- http://www.ohchr.org/Documents/Publications/DimensionsRacismen.pdf/

109. Women are inferior to men in the Quran by James M. Arlandson - http://www.answeringislam.org/Authors/Arlandson/women_inferior.htm

110. "Through the Looking Glass: What Did the Buddha Think of Women?" https://bhikkhucintita.wordpress.com/home/topics-in-the-dharma/uposatha-1272012/

111. "Through the Looking Glass: What Did the Buddha Think of Women?" https://bhikkhucintita.wordpress.com/home/topics-in-the-dharma/uposatha-1272012/

112. Judaism 101; The Role of Women; http://www.jewfaq.org/women.htm/

113. Harvard Business Review, Desperately Seeking Synergy by Michael Goold & Andrew Campbell

114. The Atlantic; Most American Christians Believe They're Victims of Discrimination by Emma Green – 6/30/16 https://www.theatlantic.com/politics/archive/2016/06/the-christians-who-believe-theyre-being-persecuted-in-america/488468//

115. Pew Social Trends; Take this Job and Love It- www.pewsocialtrends.org/2009/09/17/take-this-job-and-love-it/

116. The Huffington Post, The Problem with Political Correctness by BJ Gallagher. 4/27/13-

117. AJC; Anti-Semitism – News updated 2/17 - http://www.huffingtonpost.com/bj-gallagher/the- problem-political-correctness_b_2746663.html

118. Written by Dolly Parton and produced by Gregg Perry; Released November 29, 1980, Recorded RCA Studios, Nashville; 1980

119. GLOBAL PRIVATE EQUITY REPORT, 2015, Bain & Co.- http://www.bain.com/publications/articles/global-private-equity-report-2015.aspx/

120. Huffington Post, The Changing Business of Black Hair, a Potentially $500b Industry by Antonia Opiah http://www.huffingtonpost.com/antonia-opiah/the-changing-business-of-_b_4650819.html/

121. BET; African-American Women Rate Heavier Body Types as Attractive, Study Says- http://www.bet.com/news/health/2014/05/22/young-african-american-women-rate-heavier-body-types-as-attractive-study-says.html/

122. "This Land Is Your Land" Song by Woody Guthrie Published 1945 Recorded 1944 Writer(s) Woody Guthrie

123. American Bar Association (ABA), Political Election Issues in the Workplace; Webinar - http://shop.americanbar.org http://shop.americanbar.org/

124. Pew Research Center; After decades of GOP support, Cubans shifting toward the Democratic Party by Jens Manuel Krogstad- http://www.pewresearch.org/fact-tank/2014/06/24/after-decades-of-gop-support-cubans-shifting-toward-the-democratic-party/

125. Jerusalem Center for Public Affairs, Are American Jews Becoming Republican? Insights into Jewish Political Behavior by Steven Windmueller- http://www.jcpa.org/jl/vp509.htm/

126. Republican Party (United States) | Open Access articles | Open Access /research.omicsgroup.org in-depth/ Republican Party _ (United States) http://research.omicsgroup.org/index.php/Republican_Party_(United_States)/

127. How America Changed During Barack Obama's Presidency by Michael Dimock; Pew Research Center- http://www.pewresearch.org/2017/01/10/how-america-changed-during-barack-obamas-presidency/

128. The Atlantic; My President Was Black by Ta-Nehisi-Coates- https://www.theatlantic.com/magazine/archive/ 2017/01/my-president-was-black/508793/

129. CBS News; Tea Party Supporters, Who Are They and What They Believe by Brian Montopoli - http://www.cbsnews.com/news/tea-party-supporters-who-they-are-and-what-they-believe/

130. Barack Obama: Adaptable Team Stays on Message While Using Social Networking to Build Voter Roles by Ken Wheaton, *Advertising Age*, October 17, 2008, http://adage.com/article/special-report-marketer-of-the-year/barack-obama/131757/

131. The New American Center: Why Our Nation Isn't as Divided as We Think," by Tony Dokoupil, October 15, 2013- http://www.nbcnews.com/news/other/new-american-center-why-our-nation-isnt-divided-we-think/

132. "7 Marketing Lessons Businesses Can Learn from Obama," by Bruce Newman, Business.com, January 15, 2016, http://www.business.com/marketing/

133. Milkin Institute, Global Conference, 2013, http://www.milkeninstitute.org/

134. Esquire/NBC Survey, NBC News; "The New American Center: Why our nation isn't as divided as we think; by Tony Dokoupil – http://www.nbcnews.com/news/other/new-american-center-why-our-nation-isnt-divided-we-think-f8C1139447777/

135. Official song of the US Navy and the fight song of the US Naval Academy. It was composed in 1906 by Lt. Charles A. Zimmermann with lyrics by Midshipman Alfred Hart Miles (http://navylive.dodlive.mil/2013/01/09/lessons- learned-from- the-diversity-accountability)

136. Navy.com; "America's Navy—Navy Life/Current & Future,"

137. "Vice Adm. Moore Takes Command of Naval Sea Systems Command," by Megan Eckstein, US Naval Institute 6News (USNI News), June 10, 2016

138. "Navy Live, Lessons Learned from the Diversity Accountability Review," by Kelly Allen, January 9, 2013, blog written by VADM Kevin McCoy, commander of Naval Sea Systems Command, http://navylive.dodlive.mil/2013/01/09/lessons-learned-from-the-diversity-accountability-review/

139/140 "Navy Live, Lessons Learned from the Diversity Accountability Review," by Kelly Allen, January 9, 2013, blog written by VADM Kevin McCoy, commander of Naval Sea Systems Command, http://navylive.dodlive.mil/2013/01/09/lessons-learned-from-the-diversity-accountability-review/

141. "15 Years of Labor Shortages Predicted for the U.S. Economy," by Mitchell Hartman, Marketplace, April 19, 2016, http://www.marketplace.org/2016/04/19/world/15-years-labor-shortages-predicted-us-economy/

142. Changing Minds.org - Edward Twitchell Hall, Jr. (http://changingminds.org/explanations/culture/hallculture.htm/

143. Changing Minds.org - Edward Twitchell Hall, Jr. (http://changingminds.orgexplanationsculturehallculture.htm/ www.culture-at-work.com/highlow.html)//

144. America's Navy, Diversity Outreach in Recruiting," by Mark P. Langford, http://www.navy.mil/submit/display.asp?storyid=78915/

145. SeaPerch can be found at http://www.seaperch.org/index/

146. "America's Navy, Diversity Outreach in Recruiting," by Mark P. Langford, http://www.navy.mil/submit/display.asp?story_id=78915/.

148. "Report: Immigrants Integrating at Historic Pace," Marisa Gerstein Pineau with panel member Richard

Alba, September 23, 2015- https://www.carnegie.org/news/articles/national-academy-science-immigration-integration-interview//

149. Cato Institute; Immigrants Have Enriched American Culture and Enhanced Our Influence in the World by Daniel Griswold -https://www.cato.org/publications/commentary/immigrants-have-enriched-american-culture-enhanced-our-influence-world/

150. Immigrants Have Enriched American Culture and Enhanced Our Influence in the World," by Daniel Griswold, Cato Institute, February 18, 2002, http://www.cato.org/publications/commentary/immigrants-have-enriched-american-culture-enhanced-our-influence-world/.

151. Star Ledger; Islam is just the current American scapegoat: Opinion by Brian Regal- http://www.nj.comopinion//

152. "Four Ways Immigrants Are Crucial to the Modern American Workforce," by Esther Yu-Hsi Lee, August 30, 2013, http://thinkprogress.org//

153. Center for American Progress; The Contributions of Immigrants and Their Children to the American Workforce and Jobs of the Future by Dowell Myers, Stephen Levy and John Pitkin-___https://www.americanprogress.org/issues/immigration/reports/2013/06/19/66891/the-contributions-of-immigrants-and-their-children-to-the-american-workforce-and-jobs-of-the-future//

154. Center for Immigration Studies Welfare Use by Immigrant and Native Households, by Steven A. Camarota, September 2015, http://cis.org/Welfare-Use-Immigrant-Native-Households//

155. "Stereotypes and Prejudices: A Guide for Teachers," by Gary Grobman, http://remember.org/guide#Facts/

156. http://www.pewhispanic.org/2015/09/28/chapter-4-u-s-public-has-mixed-views-of-immigrants-and-immigration/

157. "Why Do We Need the ERA? History of the ERA," ERA Coalition,http://www.eracoalition.org/about.php.

158. Moyers & Company; The 2016 Election Exposed Deep-Seated Racism. Where Do We Go from Here by Brandon Tensley, Michael C. Richardson, and Rejane Frederick? 11/25/16- http://billmoyers.com/story/2016-election-exposed-deep-seated-racism-go//

159. "College Educated Immigrants in the U.S.," by Jie Zong and Jeanne Batalova, Migration Policy Institute, September 3, 2016, http://www.migrationpolicy.org/article/college-educated-immigrants-united-states//

160. An Aging World: 2015 International Population Reports. Issued March 2016 P95/16-1 By Wan He, Daniel Goodkind, and Paul Kowal - https://www.census.gov/content/dam/Census/library/publications/2016/demo/p95-16-f/

161/162 MPI; Migration Policy Institute, Frequently Requested Statistics on Immigrants and Immigration in the United

States by Jie Zong and Jeanne Batalova, 3/8/17- http://www.migrationpolicy.org/article/frequently-requested-statistics-immigrants-and-immigration-united-states//

163. Pew Research Center; Modern Immigration Wave Brings 59 Million to U.S., Driving Population Growth and Change Through 2065 – 9/28/15 - http://www.pewhispanic.org/2015/09/28/modern-immigration-wave-brings-59-million-to-u-s-driving-population-growth-and-change-through-2065//

164. USA Today, July 7, 2016- http://www.usatoday.com/story/tech/2015/05/05/google-raises-stakes-diversity-spending/26868359//

165. US Equal Employment Opportunity Commission, https://www.eeoc.gov/employees/coverage.cfm//

166. Gild (recruiting software), https://www.gild.com/diversity-recruiting-software//

167. "Top 10 Diversity Issues at Work," by Michelle Renee, *Houston Chronicle*, http://smallbusiness.chron.com/top-10-diversity-issues-work/

168. Workplace Harassment Still a Major Problem Experts Tell EEOC at Meeting; U.S. Equal Employment Opportunity Commission (EEOC),

169. The Loudest Voice in the Room: How the Brilliant, Bombastic Roger Ailes Built Fox News and Divided a Country, by Gabriel Sherman, Random House, 2014, retrieved March 23, 2014.

170. You Are the Message: Getting What You Want by Being Who You Are - Aug 20, 1989 by Roger Ailes and Jon Kraushar

171. New York Times, July 24, 2016.

172. Steve Denson, http://www.joandassociatesconsulting.com/topdiversityexpertsarticle.pdf/

174. The First Time I faced a Hostile Audience(Kids) by John Leguizamo; The New York Times, Culture Section – 3/26/17

175. Beatboxing is a form of vocal percussion primarily involving the art of mimicking drum machines using one's mouth, lips, tongue, and voice

www.ingramcontent.com/pod-product-compliance
Lightning Source LLC
Chambersburg PA
CBHW071422180526
45170CB00001B/185